Red Team Playbook: Building a Resilient Cyber Defense

Danyl Vassiliev

Danyl Vassiliev is a seasoned cybersecurity expert with over a decade of experience in both offensive and defensive security. With a background in information technology and a passion for protecting organizations from ever-evolving cyber threats, Danyl has dedicated his career to enhancing the resilience of cyber defense systems through effective red teaming practices.

Having worked with various industries—from finance and healthcare to government agencies—Danyl has witnessed firsthand the critical importance of understanding adversarial tactics. His hands-on experience includes leading red team engagements, developing comprehensive security strategies, and training the next generation of cybersecurity professionals. He is a firm believer in the power of collaboration between red and blue teams to create a more robust cybersecurity posture.

Danyl is also a frequent speaker at cybersecurity conferences and a contributor to various industry publications, where he shares insights on emerging threats, best practices, and innovative defense strategies. He holds multiple certifications, including Certified Information Systems Security Professional (CISSP) and Offensive Security Certified Professional (OSCP), demonstrating his commitment to continuous learning in a rapidly changing field.

In "**Red Team Playbook: Building a Resilient Cyber Defense**," Danyl combines his extensive knowledge and practical experiences to provide readers with actionable strategies and tools for developing a resilient cybersecurity framework. His goal is to empower organizations to not only anticipate and defend against cyber threats but also to cultivate a culture of security awareness that extends throughout their teams.

Through this playbook, Danyl aims to demystify the world of red teaming, offering insights that are both accessible and applicable for security professionals at all levels. Whether you are a seasoned expert or new to the field, this book will serve as a valuable resource in your journey to fortify your organization against the ever-present dangers of the digital landscape.

In today's digital landscape, the threat of cyberattacks looms larger than ever. Organizations of all sizes face an ever-evolving array of adversaries seeking to exploit vulnerabilities, steal sensitive information, and disrupt operations. As the frequency and sophistication of these attacks continue to rise, the importance of a robust cybersecurity strategy cannot be overstated. However, building an effective defense goes beyond implementing firewalls and antivirus software; it requires a proactive and holistic approach that anticipates threats before they materialize.

This is where red teaming comes into play.

"**Red Team Playbook: Building a Resilient Cyber Defense**" serves as a comprehensive guide to understanding and implementing red teaming methodologies. Red teaming, the practice of simulating real-world attacks to test the effectiveness of an organization's security posture, empowers teams to identify weaknesses and enhance their defenses. It is not just about finding vulnerabilities; it is about fostering a culture of security awareness and continuous improvement.

In this book, you will discover the principles of red teaming, the tactics employed by adversaries, and the strategies to build a resilient cyber defense. Each chapter delves into essential topics, from assembling a skilled red team and planning effective engagements to analyzing findings and creating actionable reports. You will also learn about the critical collaboration between red and blue teams, ensuring that defensive strategies are informed by real-world scenarios and insights.

Whether you are a cybersecurity professional, a decision-maker in your organization, or someone interested in understanding the complexities of cyber defense, this book offers valuable insights and practical guidance. With a focus on actionable strategies and real-world applications, "Red Team Playbook" aims to equip you with the knowledge and tools necessary to anticipate, defend against, and respond to cyber threats.

As you embark on this journey through the pages of this book, remember that building a resilient cyber defense is not a one-time effort; it is an ongoing commitment to learning, adapting, and improving. Together, let us strengthen our defenses and foster a safer digital environment for all.

Welcome to the world of red teaming—let's get started!

1. Introduction to Red Teaming

In an era where cyber threats are increasingly sophisticated and persistent, organizations must adopt a proactive approach to security. Traditional defenses, while essential, are no longer sufficient to combat the diverse and evolving tactics employed by adversaries. This is where red teaming comes into play.

In this chapter, we will explore the concept of red teaming—its definition, objectives, and historical context. We'll delve into the fundamental principles that underpin red teaming efforts and discuss how it serves as a critical component in identifying vulnerabilities and enhancing an organization's security posture. By simulating real-world attack scenarios, red teams provide invaluable insights that empower organizations to bolster their defenses.

Join us as we lay the groundwork for understanding the vital role of red teaming in today's cybersecurity landscape, setting the stage for the strategies and methodologies we will discuss in the chapters to come.

1.1. Defining Red Teaming

In the ever-evolving landscape of cybersecurity, organizations are increasingly challenged by sophisticated threats from various adversaries. To effectively combat these threats, it is essential to adopt a proactive approach to security. One such approach is red teaming, a strategic method that simulates real-world attacks to identify vulnerabilities and enhance the overall security posture of an organization.

Understanding Red Teaming

At its core, red teaming is the practice of emulating the tactics, techniques, and procedures (TTPs) used by actual adversaries to test the effectiveness of an organization's security measures. The term "red team" originates from military exercises, where a "red team" plays the role of the enemy, challenging the "blue team," or friendly forces, to prepare for and defend against potential attacks. This methodology has been adapted for cybersecurity to provide organizations with a realistic perspective on their defenses.

Unlike traditional penetration testing, which often focuses on specific vulnerabilities or configurations, red teaming takes a more holistic approach. Red team engagements aim to simulate the complete attack lifecycle, from reconnaissance and initial exploitation to lateral movement and data exfiltration. By doing so, red teams provide organizations with insights not only into technical vulnerabilities but also into organizational processes, human behavior, and response capabilities.

Key Objectives of Red Teaming

The primary objectives of red teaming can be distilled into several key areas:

Identifying Vulnerabilities: One of the foremost goals of red teaming is to uncover vulnerabilities in an organization's defenses. This includes technical weaknesses, misconfigurations, and gaps in security controls that may be exploited by adversaries.

Testing Incident Response: Red teaming assesses how well an organization's incident response team detects, responds to, and mitigates potential attacks. This includes evaluating communication protocols, decision-making processes, and the overall readiness of the team to handle real-world incidents.

Enhancing Security Awareness: By simulating real attacks, red teams help organizations improve their security awareness culture. Employees at all levels become more informed about potential threats and better understand their roles in maintaining security.

Validating Security Controls: Red teams help organizations evaluate the effectiveness of existing security measures. By testing controls in a realistic environment, organizations can determine if their defenses are adequate or need improvement.

Fostering Collaboration: Red teaming encourages collaboration between security teams, particularly between red (offensive) and blue (defensive) teams. This collaboration fosters knowledge sharing and helps both teams understand each other's perspectives and challenges.

The Red Teaming Process

The process of red teaming typically consists of several key phases:

Planning and Scoping: Before any engagement begins, red teams work with organizational stakeholders to define the scope and objectives of the exercise. This includes identifying critical assets, establishing boundaries, and ensuring compliance with legal and ethical standards.

Reconnaissance: In this phase, red teams gather information about the target organization, including its network architecture, employee details, and potential entry points. This intelligence is crucial for crafting realistic attack scenarios.

Exploitation: Armed with reconnaissance data, red teams attempt to exploit identified vulnerabilities. This phase may involve using various attack techniques, such as social engineering, phishing, or exploiting software vulnerabilities, to gain initial access.

Post-Exploitation: Once inside the target environment, red teams often engage in lateral movement, seeking to access sensitive data or systems. They assess the organization's detection capabilities during this phase and gather evidence of their activities.

Analysis and Reporting: After the engagement, red teams conduct a thorough analysis of their findings, including the vulnerabilities exploited, the success of the attack vectors used, and the organization's response. This analysis is compiled into a comprehensive report that includes actionable recommendations for improving security.

Debriefing: Finally, red teams conduct debriefing sessions with stakeholders to discuss findings, lessons learned, and strategies for enhancing defenses. These sessions foster collaboration between red and blue teams and promote a culture of continuous improvement.

The Role of Red Teams in Cybersecurity

The role of red teams in cybersecurity extends beyond merely identifying vulnerabilities. By simulating real-world attack scenarios, red teams play a vital role in helping organizations strengthen their defenses against a multitude of threats. They provide organizations with a clear understanding of their security posture and highlight areas for improvement.

Proactive Defense: Red teaming embodies a proactive approach to cybersecurity. Rather than waiting for an actual attack to occur, organizations can leverage red teaming to anticipate potential threats and mitigate them before they can be exploited.

Real-World Perspective: The insights provided by red teams are invaluable. They offer organizations a real-world perspective on the tactics used by actual adversaries, helping security teams better understand how to defend against them.

Continuous Improvement: Cybersecurity is not a one-time effort; it requires ongoing vigilance and adaptation. Red teaming encourages organizations to adopt a mindset of continuous improvement, regularly reassessing their defenses and strategies in light of new threats.

Cultural Shift: Implementing red teaming can help shift an organization's culture toward a more security-conscious mindset. When employees understand the tactics employed by adversaries, they are more likely to adopt security best practices in their day-to-day activities.

Challenges and Considerations

While red teaming offers numerous benefits, organizations must also consider several challenges when implementing these programs:

Resource Constraints: Building a red team requires investment in skilled personnel, tools, and technologies. Organizations must allocate resources effectively to ensure successful engagements.

Managing Expectations: It is essential for organizations to set realistic expectations for red team engagements. Stakeholders should understand that the goal is to identify vulnerabilities, not to create a hostile environment.

Legal and Ethical Concerns: Red teams must operate within legal and ethical boundaries. Organizations must ensure that engagements comply with relevant laws and regulations and that all parties involved are informed and consent to the testing.

Integration with Blue Teams: Successful red teaming relies on collaboration with blue teams. Organizations should foster an environment where both teams can work together to improve security rather than creating an adversarial dynamic.

Defining red teaming is crucial for organizations seeking to enhance their cybersecurity posture. By emulating real-world threats and providing actionable insights, red teams play a vital role in identifying vulnerabilities, validating security controls, and fostering a culture of collaboration and continuous improvement. As the threat landscape continues to evolve, the importance of red teaming will only grow, serving as a critical component of a proactive and resilient cybersecurity strategy. By understanding and embracing red teaming, organizations can better prepare themselves to face the challenges of the digital age and safeguard their assets against an array of cyber threats.

1.2. Historical Context and Evolution

Red teaming has its roots in military strategy, where the concepts of offense and defense have long been critical to national security. The practice of simulating enemy tactics to prepare for conflict can be traced back to ancient military exercises. However, the application of red teaming in cybersecurity is a more recent development, evolving in response to the rapid advancement of technology and the increasing sophistication of cyber threats. This chapter will explore the historical context and evolution of red teaming, highlighting its origins, development, and current significance in the cybersecurity landscape.

Origins in Military Strategy

The concept of red teaming emerged from military training exercises designed to prepare forces for combat. During these exercises, a "red team" would simulate the enemy, employing tactics and strategies that the opposing "blue team" would need to counter. This practice aimed to enhance the operational readiness of military units, testing their ability to adapt to and overcome adversarial tactics.

Early Military Exercises: The practice of war games can be traced back to ancient civilizations. For instance, the Chinese military strategist Sun Tzu advocated for understanding one's enemy as a critical component of successful warfare in his seminal work, The Art of War. Similarly, the Prussian military used war games in the 19th century to prepare for real battles by simulating various scenarios.

The Cold War Era: The formalization of red teaming as a military strategy took shape during the Cold War. In response to the emerging threat of nuclear warfare, military leaders recognized the need to evaluate their strategies against potential Soviet tactics. The U.S. military began to employ red teams to identify weaknesses in their defenses and prepare for various conflict scenarios. This marked the beginning of a structured approach to red teaming, emphasizing the importance of adversarial thinking.

The Transition to Cybersecurity

As technology advanced and the Internet became a crucial part of modern society, the focus of red teaming began to shift toward cybersecurity. The increasing reliance on digital infrastructure exposed organizations to new and evolving threats, prompting a need for innovative strategies to defend against cyber attacks.

The Rise of Cyber Threats: The late 20th and early 21st centuries witnessed a surge in cyber threats, from hackers exploiting system vulnerabilities to organized cybercriminal enterprises. High-profile incidents, such as the Morris Worm in 1988 and the SolarWinds breach in 2020, highlighted the vulnerabilities of organizations and underscored the necessity of robust cybersecurity measures.

Emergence of Red Teaming in Cybersecurity: In the early 2000s, organizations began adopting red teaming as a method to assess their cybersecurity defenses. The National Security Agency (NSA) and the Department of Defense (DoD) were among the first to implement red teaming within their cybersecurity frameworks. These initiatives aimed to mimic the tactics of adversaries, providing valuable insights into vulnerabilities and areas for improvement.

Development of Frameworks and Methodologies

As red teaming gained traction in the cybersecurity field, various frameworks and methodologies emerged to guide practitioners in conducting effective engagements. This development facilitated a more structured and standardized approach to red teaming.

The Penetration Testing Framework: Early red teaming efforts often overlapped with traditional penetration testing methodologies. Both approaches aimed to identify vulnerabilities, but red teaming emphasized simulating real-world attack scenarios over simple vulnerability assessments. Frameworks like the OWASP Testing Guide and the PTES (Penetration Testing Execution Standard) emerged to provide guidelines for both penetration testers and red teamers.

Advent of the MITRE ATT&CK Framework: In 2013, the MITRE Corporation introduced the ATT&CK (Adversarial Tactics, Techniques, and Common Knowledge) framework. This comprehensive matrix categorizes various tactics and techniques used by adversaries during attacks, providing red teams with a valuable resource for emulating real-world threats. The framework has become a cornerstone in the field, guiding red team engagements and enhancing the effectiveness of simulations.

The Role of Technology in Evolution

The evolution of red teaming has been significantly influenced by advancements in technology. The increasing complexity of networks, the proliferation of cloud computing, and the emergence of new attack vectors have all shaped red teaming practices.

Automation and Tools: The development of sophisticated tools and automation has transformed red teaming engagements. Tools such as Metasploit, Cobalt Strike, and Burp Suite enable red teamers to conduct thorough assessments efficiently. Automation allows teams to focus on more complex attack scenarios, improving the overall effectiveness of red teaming efforts.

Incorporation of Artificial Intelligence: The rise of artificial intelligence (AI) and machine learning has begun to impact red teaming practices. AI-powered tools can analyze vast amounts of data, identify patterns, and predict potential vulnerabilities, enhancing the effectiveness of reconnaissance efforts. As technology continues to evolve, red teams will likely leverage AI to stay ahead of emerging threats.

Current Significance and Future Trends

Today, red teaming is recognized as a vital component of modern cybersecurity strategies. Organizations across various sectors, including government, finance, healthcare, and critical infrastructure, are increasingly adopting red teaming to assess their defenses and improve their security postures.

Regulatory Compliance: Regulatory bodies are beginning to recognize the importance of red teaming in ensuring cybersecurity compliance. Organizations that engage in red teaming demonstrate a commitment to proactive security measures, which can enhance their standing with regulators and stakeholders.

Adaptation to New Threats: As cyber threats continue to evolve, red teams must adapt their methodologies to address emerging challenges. Trends such as the rise of ransomware, supply chain attacks, and the increasing sophistication of state-sponsored threats necessitate continuous evolution in red teaming practices. The ability to simulate these complex scenarios will be crucial for organizations seeking to maintain resilience against advanced threats.

Collaboration Between Red and Blue Teams: The future of red teaming will likely involve increased collaboration between red and blue teams. Organizations are beginning to recognize that a cooperative approach—where red teams provide insights and recommendations while blue teams implement defenses—can lead to a more robust cybersecurity posture. This collaboration fosters a culture of continuous improvement and shared learning.

The historical context and evolution of red teaming reflect a journey from military strategy to a critical component of modern cybersecurity practices. As organizations face an increasingly complex and hostile cyber threat landscape, red teaming provides a proactive approach to identifying vulnerabilities and enhancing defenses. By understanding the origins and development of red teaming, cybersecurity professionals can appreciate its significance and leverage it effectively to safeguard their organizations against evolving threats. As technology continues to advance and cyber adversaries become more sophisticated, the importance of red teaming will only grow, ensuring its place as a cornerstone of a resilient cybersecurity strategy.

1.3. Key Objectives and Outcomes

Red teaming has become a pivotal strategy in the realm of cybersecurity, offering organizations a proactive means of assessing their security posture against real-world threats. By simulating adversarial tactics, red teams help identify vulnerabilities and enhance defenses, ultimately strengthening an organization's ability to withstand cyber attacks. In this chapter, we will explore the key objectives of red teaming and the desired outcomes that organizations seek to achieve through these engagements.

Key Objectives of Red Teaming

The objectives of red teaming can be categorized into several fundamental areas that collectively contribute to an organization's cybersecurity resilience:

Vulnerability Identification

- **Assessment of Security Posture**: The primary goal of red teaming is to uncover vulnerabilities within an organization's systems, networks, and applications. By simulating real-world attacks, red teams can identify weaknesses that may be exploited by actual adversaries.
- **Holistic Approach**: Unlike traditional penetration testing, which often focuses on specific vulnerabilities, red teaming adopts a more comprehensive approach. This includes evaluating not only technical vulnerabilities but also processes, policies, and human factors that may contribute to security gaps.

Testing Incident Response Capabilities

- **Realistic Scenarios**: Red team engagements are designed to simulate realistic attack scenarios that test an organization's incident response capabilities. By assessing how well an organization can detect, respond to, and mitigate attacks, red teams provide insights into the effectiveness of existing response protocols.

- **Tabletop Exercises**: Red teams may conduct tabletop exercises alongside incident response teams to evaluate decision-making processes during a simulated attack. This allows organizations to identify areas for improvement in their response strategies and communication protocols.

Enhancing Security Awareness and Culture

- **Employee Training**: Red teaming plays a crucial role in raising security awareness among employees. By exposing staff to simulated attacks, organizations can foster a culture of vigilance and proactive security practices. Employees become more knowledgeable about potential threats and their roles in preventing breaches.
- **Cross-Departmental Collaboration**: Engaging various departments, including IT, operations, and management, in red teaming exercises encourages a unified approach to security. This collaborative environment enhances overall organizational resilience.

Validating Security Controls

- **Effectiveness of Defenses**: Red teaming provides organizations with a means to evaluate the effectiveness of their existing security controls. By testing these controls against simulated attacks, red teams can identify weaknesses and recommend improvements to enhance defenses.
- **Continuous Improvement**: Organizations can use insights gained from red team engagements to refine their security strategies continuously. This iterative process ensures that defenses remain adaptive and effective against evolving threats.

Fostering Collaboration Between Red and Blue Teams

- **Knowledge Sharing**: One of the key objectives of red teaming is to foster collaboration between red (offensive) and blue (defensive) teams. By working together, both teams can share insights, improve communication, and develop a deeper understanding of each other's perspectives and challenges.
- **Continuous Learning**: This collaboration promotes a culture of continuous learning, where red teams provide feedback on the effectiveness of blue team defenses, leading to ongoing enhancements in security practices.

Desired Outcomes of Red Teaming

The objectives of red teaming ultimately aim to achieve specific outcomes that contribute to an organization's overall cybersecurity resilience. These outcomes can be categorized as follows:

Improved Security Posture

- **Identification of Weaknesses**: By identifying vulnerabilities and weaknesses, red teaming helps organizations improve their security posture. This enhanced posture reduces the risk of successful attacks and strengthens defenses against a variety of threats.
- **Actionable Recommendations**: The insights gained from red team engagements lead to actionable recommendations for remediation. Organizations can prioritize addressing critical vulnerabilities, ensuring a more effective allocation of resources.

Enhanced Incident Response

- **Improved Response Time**: By testing incident response capabilities through realistic attack simulations, organizations can enhance their ability to detect and respond to threats more quickly. This improved response time is critical in minimizing damage during actual incidents.
- **Refined Protocols**: Red teaming provides organizations with the opportunity to refine their incident response protocols based on lessons learned from simulations. This leads to more effective communication, coordination, and decision-making during real-world attacks.

Increased Security Awareness

- **Employee Engagement**: Engaging employees in red teaming exercises fosters a greater understanding of cybersecurity risks. Employees become more vigilant and proactive in identifying potential threats, contributing to a culture of security awareness.
- **Training Opportunities**: Red teaming can serve as a training tool for employees, providing them with hands-on experience in recognizing and responding to security threats. This practical knowledge empowers staff to take an active role in maintaining security.

Validation and Optimization of Security Controls

- **Effectiveness Testing**: Organizations can validate the effectiveness of their security controls through red teaming. By simulating attacks, they can determine whether existing defenses can withstand real-world threats.
- **Optimized Security Strategies**: The insights gained from red team engagements lead to optimized security strategies. Organizations can allocate resources more effectively, ensuring that critical vulnerabilities are addressed promptly.

Strengthened Collaboration and Communication

- **Synergy Between Teams**: Red teaming encourages collaboration between red and blue teams, leading to improved synergy and communication. This collaborative environment fosters a shared understanding of security challenges and enhances the overall effectiveness of security efforts.
- **Cultural Shift**: The integration of red teaming into an organization's cybersecurity strategy can facilitate a cultural shift toward a more proactive and security-focused mindset. Employees at all levels become more aware of the importance of cybersecurity and their roles in safeguarding assets.

Red teaming serves as a vital strategy for organizations seeking to enhance their cybersecurity posture and resilience against evolving threats. By focusing on key objectives such as vulnerability identification, incident response testing, and security awareness, red teams provide organizations with valuable insights and actionable recommendations. The desired outcomes of red teaming, including improved security posture, enhanced incident response capabilities, and strengthened collaboration, collectively contribute to a robust and adaptive cybersecurity strategy. As organizations continue to navigate the complexities of the digital landscape, red teaming will remain an essential component of their efforts to safeguard critical assets and mitigate cyber risks.

2. Understanding the Threat Landscape

In order to effectively defend against cyber threats, it is crucial to have a deep understanding of the landscape in which these threats exist. The threat landscape is dynamic and complex, characterized by a myriad of adversaries, techniques, and motivations that continuously evolve. From state-sponsored actors to cybercriminals and hacktivists, the range of potential threats is vast and varied.

In this chapter, we will examine the current cyber threat landscape, focusing on the tactics, techniques, and procedures (TTPs) employed by various adversaries. We will also explore the factors driving these threats, such as geopolitical tensions, economic incentives, and technological advancements. By analyzing notable case studies of cyber attacks, we aim to illustrate the real-world implications of these threats and underscore the necessity for organizations to stay informed and vigilant.

As we delve into this critical subject, you will gain insights that will not only help you understand the challenges at hand but also inform your red teaming efforts and the development of more robust security strategies. Understanding the threat landscape is the first step in anticipating and mitigating risks, paving the way for a more resilient cyber defense.

2.1. Current Cyber Threats and Trends

In an increasingly digital world, organizations are facing a multitude of cyber threats that are evolving in complexity and scale. As technology continues to advance, so too do the methods employed by cyber adversaries. Understanding the current cyber threats and trends is essential for organizations looking to bolster their defenses and effectively respond to potential attacks. This chapter explores the prevailing cyber threats, emerging trends, and the implications they hold for businesses and individuals alike.

Overview of Current Cyber Threats

Cyber threats can take many forms, each targeting different aspects of an organization's infrastructure, data, or operations. Some of the most prominent cyber threats today include:

Ransomware Attacks

- **Description**: Ransomware has become one of the most notorious cyber threats, where attackers encrypt an organization's data and demand a ransom for its release. In some cases, attackers may also threaten to publish sensitive information if the ransom is not paid.
- **Impact**: Ransomware attacks can lead to significant financial losses, operational disruptions, and reputational damage. Organizations that are unable to recover their data may face lengthy downtime and substantial recovery costs.

Phishing and Social Engineering

- **Description**: Phishing involves using deceptive emails or messages to trick individuals into revealing sensitive information, such as usernames, passwords, or financial data. Social engineering encompasses a broader range of tactics, including impersonating trusted sources to manipulate victims into taking harmful actions.
- **Impact**: Successful phishing attacks can lead to unauthorized access to systems, data breaches, and financial losses. As attackers become more sophisticated, these tactics are increasingly difficult to detect.

Supply Chain Attacks

- **Description**: Supply chain attacks target vulnerabilities within an organization's supply chain, compromising third-party vendors to gain access to larger targets. Notable examples include the SolarWinds and Kaseya breaches, where attackers infiltrated trusted software providers to distribute malicious code.
- **Impact**: These attacks can have far-reaching consequences, affecting multiple organizations within a supply chain. The complexity of modern supply chains makes them an attractive target for adversaries seeking to bypass traditional defenses.

Distributed Denial of Service (DDoS) Attacks

- **Description**: DDoS attacks involve overwhelming a target's network or services with a flood of traffic, rendering them inaccessible to legitimate users. Attackers may use botnets—networks of compromised devices—to amplify the attack's scale.
- **Impact**: DDoS attacks can disrupt operations, resulting in downtime and loss of revenue. Organizations may also incur significant costs in mitigating these attacks and restoring services.

Advanced Persistent Threats (APTs)

- **Description**: APTs are prolonged and targeted cyber attacks, typically carried out by well-funded and organized threat actors, such as nation-states. These attacks often involve stealthy techniques to maintain persistent access to a target's network over an extended period.
- **Impact**: APTs can lead to extensive data breaches, intellectual property theft, and long-term damage to an organization's reputation. The stealthy nature of these attacks makes them challenging to detect and remediate.

Internet of Things (IoT) Vulnerabilities

- **Description**: As IoT devices proliferate, they introduce new vulnerabilities that adversaries can exploit. Many IoT devices lack robust security measures, making them easy targets for attackers seeking to compromise networks.
- **Impact**: Compromised IoT devices can serve as entry points for broader attacks, allowing adversaries to gain access to sensitive systems and data. Additionally, the sheer number of IoT devices increases the attack surface for organizations.

Emerging Trends in Cybersecurity

As cyber threats evolve, several trends are shaping the cybersecurity landscape. Understanding these trends is crucial for organizations looking to stay ahead of potential attacks.

Increased Adoption of Zero Trust Architecture

- **Overview**: The zero trust security model operates on the principle of "never trust, always verify." This approach requires continuous authentication and validation of users and devices, regardless of their location within or outside the network.
- **Implications**: Adopting a zero trust architecture can significantly enhance an organization's security posture by reducing the risk of unauthorized access and lateral movement within networks. Organizations are increasingly implementing micro-segmentation, multifactor authentication, and strict access controls as part of this model.

Shift to Cloud Security

- **Overview**: As organizations migrate to cloud environments, the need for robust cloud security measures has become paramount. Cloud service providers are

enhancing their security offerings, but organizations must also take responsibility for securing their data and applications in the cloud.
- **Implications**: The shift to cloud security emphasizes the importance of shared responsibility models, where organizations must ensure they implement adequate security controls, monitor configurations, and conduct regular assessments to protect cloud-based assets.

Integration of Artificial Intelligence and Machine Learning

- **Overview**: AI and machine learning technologies are increasingly being utilized in cybersecurity to enhance threat detection, response, and analysis. These technologies can analyze vast amounts of data, identify patterns, and predict potential threats in real time.
- **Implications**: The integration of AI in cybersecurity enables organizations to respond more quickly to incidents, automate repetitive tasks, and improve overall efficiency. However, adversaries are also using AI to develop more sophisticated attacks, leading to an ongoing arms race in the cybersecurity landscape.

Rise of Cyber Insurance

- **Overview**: As cyber threats become more prevalent, organizations are increasingly turning to cyber insurance to mitigate financial losses associated with breaches and attacks. Cyber insurance policies can cover a range of costs, including incident response, legal fees, and data recovery.
- **Implications**: The rise of cyber insurance underscores the importance of risk management in cybersecurity strategies. Organizations must carefully evaluate their risk exposure and consider how insurance can complement their security measures.

Regulatory Compliance and Data Privacy

- **Overview**: Regulatory requirements related to data privacy and security are becoming more stringent. Laws such as the General Data Protection Regulation (GDPR) and the California Consumer Privacy Act (CCPA) impose significant obligations on organizations regarding data protection and breach notification.
- **Implications**: Organizations must prioritize compliance as part of their cybersecurity strategies, ensuring they have adequate controls in place to protect sensitive data and meet regulatory requirements. Failure to comply can result in substantial fines and reputational damage.

Increased Focus on Supply Chain Security

- **Overview**: The growing recognition of supply chain vulnerabilities has led organizations to prioritize supply chain security. This trend emphasizes the need for organizations to assess the security posture of their vendors and partners.
- **Implications**: Organizations must conduct thorough risk assessments and due diligence when selecting vendors, ensuring they implement appropriate security measures. Additionally, organizations are increasingly adopting best practices for monitoring and managing supply chain risks.

Understanding the current cyber threats and trends is essential for organizations seeking to strengthen their cybersecurity defenses. The landscape is marked by an array of threats, from ransomware and phishing to supply chain attacks and IoT vulnerabilities. At the same time, emerging trends, such as zero trust architecture, cloud security, and the integration of AI, are reshaping the way organizations approach cybersecurity.

By staying informed about these threats and trends, organizations can adopt proactive measures to protect their assets and respond effectively to potential attacks. This ongoing awareness is critical for navigating the complexities of the digital landscape and ensuring long-term cybersecurity resilience. As cyber adversaries continue to adapt and evolve, organizations must remain vigilant and agile in their cybersecurity strategies, continuously assessing and enhancing their defenses to address the dynamic threat landscape.

2.2. Adversary Tactics, Techniques, and Procedures (TTPs)

In the ever-evolving landscape of cybersecurity, understanding the tactics, techniques, and procedures (TTPs) used by adversaries is crucial for organizations looking to fortify their defenses. TTPs provide insight into how attackers operate, allowing security teams to anticipate, detect, and respond to potential threats more effectively. This chapter explores the concept of TTPs, their significance in cybersecurity, and examples of common tactics and techniques employed by cyber adversaries.

Understanding Tactics, Techniques, and Procedures

Tactics, Techniques, and Procedures (TTPs) are a framework used to describe the behavior and methodologies of cyber adversaries.

Tactics refer to the high-level goals or objectives that attackers aim to achieve during an operation. These can range from stealing data and disrupting services to establishing persistence within a network.

Techniques are the general methods or strategies used to achieve these tactical goals. Techniques provide a broader context and may involve a variety of specific tools and methods to exploit vulnerabilities or gain unauthorized access.

Procedures are the specific implementations of techniques, including the actual tools, scripts, and configurations that adversaries use during an attack. Procedures offer a detailed understanding of how a particular technique is executed in practice.

By analyzing TTPs, cybersecurity professionals can develop a more comprehensive understanding of adversary behavior, which in turn informs their defensive strategies and incident response plans.

The Significance of TTPs in Cybersecurity

Threat Intelligence

TTPs play a vital role in threat intelligence by providing organizations with actionable insights into how attackers operate. Understanding the TTPs of known threat actors enables organizations to tailor their defenses to mitigate specific risks.

Proactive Defense

By studying adversary TTPs, organizations can identify potential vulnerabilities and weak points in their systems before they are exploited. This proactive approach allows for the implementation of security measures that can thwart attacks at various stages of the attack lifecycle.

Incident Response

When an incident occurs, having a clear understanding of adversary TTPs can streamline the incident response process. Security teams can quickly identify the tools and methods used by attackers, allowing for a more efficient and targeted response.

Threat Modeling

TTPs can be integrated into threat modeling exercises to help organizations assess their risk exposure. By mapping potential adversary tactics to their specific environment, organizations can better prioritize their security investments and focus on the most critical areas.

Common Adversary Tactics and Techniques

To illustrate the diverse range of TTPs employed by adversaries, this section outlines several common tactics and associated techniques.

Initial Access

- **Phishing**: Attackers often use phishing emails to trick users into clicking malicious links or downloading infected attachments, leading to credential theft or malware installation.
- **Exploitation of Public-Facing Applications**: Adversaries may target vulnerabilities in web applications to gain initial access. Techniques include SQL injection, cross-site scripting (XSS), and remote code execution.
- **Supply Chain Compromise**: Attackers can infiltrate organizations by compromising third-party vendors or service providers, allowing them to leverage trusted relationships for initial access.

Execution

- **Command and Scripting Interpreter**: Attackers may use command-line interfaces, PowerShell, or scripts to execute malicious commands on compromised systems.
- **Scheduled Task/Job**: Adversaries can establish persistence by creating scheduled tasks or cron jobs that execute malicious scripts at specified intervals.
- **Application Layer Protocol**: Using application layer protocols like HTTP or DNS, attackers can communicate with compromised systems, facilitating command and control.

Persistence

- **Registry Run Keys/Startup Folder**: Adversaries often modify registry keys or place malicious programs in startup folders to ensure they execute every time the system starts.
- **Web Shells**: Attackers can upload web shells to compromised servers, providing them with a backdoor for future access.

- **Scheduled Tasks**: Creating scheduled tasks can maintain persistence on a system, allowing attackers to regain access even after reboots or system updates.

Privilege Escalation

- **Exploitation of Vulnerabilities**: Attackers may exploit known vulnerabilities in software or operating systems to escalate their privileges within a network.
- **Credential Dumping**: Techniques such as extracting passwords from memory, registry, or configuration files can provide attackers with the necessary credentials to elevate their access rights.
- **Bypassing User Account Control (UAC):** Adversaries may attempt to bypass UAC mechanisms to execute malicious code with elevated privileges.

Defense Evasion

- **Obfuscation**: Attackers can use various techniques to obfuscate malicious code, making it difficult for security solutions to detect and analyze.
- **Disabling Security Tools**: Adversaries may attempt to disable antivirus or endpoint detection and response (EDR) tools to avoid detection during an attack.
- **File and Directory Permissions Modification**: By changing file permissions, attackers can hide malicious files and avoid scrutiny.

Credential Access

- **Credential Dumping**: Techniques like Mimikatz can extract stored credentials from memory, allowing attackers to gather usernames and passwords.
- **Brute Force**: Adversaries may use brute force methods to guess passwords and gain unauthorized access to accounts or systems.
- **Keylogging**: Installing keyloggers enables attackers to capture keystrokes, revealing sensitive information such as passwords and personal data.

Discovery

- **Network Scanning**: Adversaries often conduct reconnaissance using tools to scan networks for vulnerabilities, open ports, and active devices.
- **Account Discovery**: Attackers may enumerate accounts on a system to identify high-value targets and gather intelligence on users.
- **System Information Discovery**: Gathering information about the operating system, software, and configurations can help adversaries formulate their attack strategies.

Lateral Movement

- **Pass-the-Hash**: Attackers may exploit the hash of a user's password to authenticate to other systems without needing the plaintext password.
- **Remote Services**: Using legitimate remote administration tools, attackers can move laterally within a network and compromise additional systems.
- **Windows Admin Shares**: Adversaries can use Windows administrative shares (e.g., C$) to access files on remote systems and propagate malware.

Collection

- **Data from Information Repositories**: Attackers may target databases, file shares, and content management systems to collect sensitive data.
- **Data Staging**: Compromised data is often staged in a central location before exfiltration, making it easier for attackers to gather and move large quantities of data.
- **Keylogging**: Capturing user input can provide attackers with sensitive data, including login credentials and personal information.

Exfiltration

- **Data Encrypted**: Attackers may encrypt sensitive data before exfiltration to avoid detection during the transfer process.
- **Exfiltration Over Command and Control Channel**: Data is often exfiltrated over established command and control channels, using protocols like HTTP/S or DNS to obfuscate the activity.
- **Use of Removable Media**: Physical devices like USB drives can be used to transfer stolen data, circumventing network monitoring.

Impact

- **Data Destruction**: In some cases, attackers may aim to destroy data, causing significant operational disruptions and financial losses.
- **Service Stop**: Disrupting services can lead to business interruptions, impacting an organization's ability to operate.
- **Data Manipulation**: Altering or manipulating data can have far-reaching consequences, affecting decision-making processes and operational integrity.

Understanding adversary tactics, techniques, and procedures (TTPs) is essential for organizations striving to enhance their cybersecurity posture. By studying the methods employed by cyber adversaries, organizations can develop proactive defenses, improve incident response capabilities, and foster a culture of security awareness. The dynamic nature of cyber threats necessitates ongoing vigilance, as adversaries continuously adapt their strategies to exploit vulnerabilities and evade detection.

By leveraging TTPs as a framework for analyzing and responding to threats, organizations can stay one step ahead of potential attackers. This proactive approach not only helps mitigate risks but also fosters a resilient security environment that can withstand the challenges posed by an ever-evolving threat landscape.

2.3. Case Studies of Notable Cyber Attacks

Cyber attacks have become increasingly sophisticated, affecting organizations across various sectors and geographies. Understanding the methods, impacts, and lessons learned from notable cyber attacks can provide valuable insights into the ever-evolving landscape of cybersecurity. This chapter presents case studies of several significant cyber attacks, highlighting the adversaries' tactics, techniques, and procedures (TTPs) used, as well as the implications for cybersecurity practices.

1. The Target Data Breach (2013)

Overview

In late 2013, Target Corporation, a leading American retailer, experienced one of the largest data breaches in history, compromising the personal and financial information of over 40 million credit and debit card customers. The breach was discovered in December, just before the holiday shopping season.

Attack Vector

The attackers gained access to Target's network through a third-party vendor, an HVAC contractor that had privileged access to Target's systems. They used phishing emails to compromise the vendor's credentials, enabling them to install malware on Target's point-of-sale (POS) terminals.

TTPs Used

- **Initial Access**: Phishing to compromise third-party vendor credentials.
- **Execution**: Installation of memory-scraping malware on POS terminals.
- **Exfiltration**: Use of encrypted traffic to send stolen card information to external servers.

Impact

- Compromise of 40 million credit and debit card numbers and 70 million records containing personal information.
- Estimated costs of over $162 million for Target, including fines, legal fees, and customer compensation.
- Significant damage to brand reputation and loss of consumer trust.

Lessons Learned

- **Third-Party Risk Management**: Organizations must ensure robust security measures are in place for third-party vendors.
- **Network Segmentation**: Implementing strict network segmentation can limit the ability of attackers to move laterally within systems.
- **Monitoring and Detection**: Continuous monitoring of network traffic can help identify unusual activities indicative of a breach.

2. The Sony Pictures Hack (2014)

Overview

In November 2014, Sony Pictures Entertainment was the victim of a major cyber attack that led to the theft and release of confidential data, including unreleased films, employee information, and internal communications.

Attack Vector

The attackers, believed to be linked to North Korea, used sophisticated spear-phishing attacks to gain access to Sony's network. Once inside, they deployed destructive malware, wiping data from many systems and making it impossible for the company to operate.

TTPs Used

- **Initial Access**: Spear-phishing emails targeting Sony employees.

- **Execution**: Deployment of the "Wiper" malware to erase data and disrupt operations.
- **Impact**: Disruption of business operations and significant data loss.

Impact

- Theft of sensitive corporate data, including executive emails and unreleased films.
- Estimated costs of $100 million in remediation and recovery efforts.
- Public relations fallout and damage to Sony's brand image.

Lessons Learned

- **Incident Response Planning**: Organizations must have a robust incident response plan to quickly address breaches and minimize damage.
- **Employee Training**: Continuous employee training on phishing and social engineering can reduce the likelihood of successful attacks.
- **Data Protection**: Implementing strong data loss prevention (DLP) measures can help protect sensitive information.

3. The Equifax Data Breach (2017)

Overview

In September 2017, Equifax, one of the largest credit reporting agencies in the United States, announced a data breach that exposed the personal information of approximately 147 million Americans, including Social Security numbers, birth dates, and addresses.

Attack Vector

The breach resulted from a vulnerability in a web application framework (Apache Struts) that Equifax failed to patch in a timely manner. Attackers exploited this vulnerability to gain access to Equifax's databases.

TTPs Used

- **Initial Access**: Exploitation of an unpatched vulnerability in Apache Struts.
- **Execution**: Use of SQL injection techniques to access sensitive databases.
- **Exfiltration**: Large-scale exfiltration of data over an extended period.

Impact

- Compromise of sensitive personal information of 147 million individuals.
- Equifax faced more than $700 million in settlements, fines, and legal fees.
- Significant reputational damage and loss of consumer trust.

Lessons Learned

- **Timely Patch Management**: Regularly updating and patching software vulnerabilities is crucial to prevent exploitation.
- **Vulnerability Management Programs**: Implementing a robust vulnerability management program can help organizations identify and remediate weaknesses proactively.
- **Data Minimization**: Organizations should only collect and retain data that is necessary for their operations, reducing the impact of potential breaches.

4. The WannaCry Ransomware Attack (2017)

Overview

In May 2017, the WannaCry ransomware attack affected hundreds of thousands of computers across 150 countries, crippling organizations and institutions, including the National Health Service (NHS) in the UK.

Attack Vector

WannaCry exploited a vulnerability in Windows systems known as EternalBlue, which was leaked from the National Security Agency (NSA). The ransomware spread rapidly through local and wide-area networks, encrypting files and demanding a ransom in Bitcoin.

TTPs Used

- **Initial Access**: Exploitation of the EternalBlue vulnerability in unpatched Windows systems.
- **Propagation**: Use of SMB (Server Message Block) protocol to spread laterally within networks.
- **Impact**: Encryption of files, leading to service disruptions and ransom demands.

Impact

- Affected over 200,000 systems worldwide, causing significant operational disruptions, particularly in healthcare.
- Estimated costs of $4 billion in damages and lost productivity.
- Highlighted vulnerabilities in outdated systems and poor patch management.

Lessons Learned

- **Regular Backups**: Regularly backing up critical data can mitigate the impact of ransomware attacks.
- **Vulnerability Management**: Organizations must prioritize patch management and vulnerability remediation to prevent exploitation of known weaknesses.
- **Incident Response Preparedness**: Developing and testing incident response plans can help organizations respond swiftly to ransomware attacks.

5. The Colonial Pipeline Ransomware Attack (2021)

Overview

In May 2021, Colonial Pipeline, a major US fuel pipeline operator, suffered a ransomware attack that forced the company to shut down operations, leading to fuel shortages across the eastern United States.

Attack Vector

The attackers gained initial access through a compromised password for a legacy VPN system that did not have multifactor authentication (MFA) enabled. Once inside the network, they deployed ransomware to encrypt systems and demanded a ransom payment.

TTPs Used

- **Initial Access**: Compromise of VPN credentials.
- **Execution**: Deployment of ransomware to encrypt critical systems.
- **Exfiltration**: Data was exfiltrated before encryption, adding pressure to pay the ransom.

Impact

- Temporary shutdown of the pipeline operations, causing widespread fuel shortages and panic buying.

- Colonial Pipeline paid approximately $4.4 million in ransom to restore operations.
- Raised awareness of the vulnerabilities in critical infrastructure and the need for improved cybersecurity measures.

Lessons Learned

- **Importance of MFA**: Implementing multifactor authentication on all access points can significantly reduce the risk of unauthorized access.
- **Critical Infrastructure Security**: Enhancing the cybersecurity posture of critical infrastructure is essential to protect against ransomware and other cyber threats.
- **Collaboration with Law Enforcement**: Organizations should establish relationships with law enforcement and cybersecurity agencies to respond effectively to cyber incidents.

The case studies presented in this chapter illustrate the diverse nature of cyber attacks and the various tactics, techniques, and procedures employed by adversaries. By examining these notable incidents, organizations can gain valuable insights into the evolving threat landscape and the importance of proactive cybersecurity measures.

Understanding the implications of these attacks reinforces the need for comprehensive cybersecurity strategies that encompass employee training, vulnerability management, incident response planning, and robust defenses against emerging threats. As cyber adversaries continue to adapt their tactics, organizations must remain vigilant and agile in their efforts to protect their assets and ensure the resilience of their operations.

3. The Anatomy of a Cyber Attack

To effectively defend against cyber threats, one must first understand the intricate mechanics of a cyber attack. Every attack unfolds in distinct phases, each characterized by specific objectives and tactics employed by the adversary. From initial reconnaissance to the ultimate exfiltration of data, comprehending these phases is essential for both identifying potential weaknesses and developing robust defensive measures.

In this chapter, we will dissect the anatomy of a cyber attack, examining the critical stages involved—from reconnaissance and scanning to exploitation and post-exploitation activities. We will explore common attack vectors, tools, and methods utilized by threat actors, shedding light on the decision-making processes that drive their actions.

By dissecting real-world examples of cyber attacks, we aim to illustrate how these phases interconnect and highlight the vulnerabilities that organizations face at each stage. This understanding not only aids in anticipating attacks but also informs the strategies and techniques employed during red team engagements. As we navigate through the anatomy of cyber attacks, you will gain valuable insights that empower you to enhance your organization's security posture and resilience against future threats.

3.1. Phases of an Attack: Reconnaissance to Execution

Understanding the phases of a cyber attack is crucial for developing effective defenses and response strategies. Each phase of an attack provides insights into the methodologies employed by adversaries, enabling organizations to better prepare for and mitigate potential threats. This chapter breaks down the typical phases of a cyber attack, from reconnaissance through execution, illustrating how attackers operate at each stage and what defensive measures can be employed to thwart their efforts.

1. Reconnaissance

Overview

Reconnaissance is the initial phase of a cyber attack, where adversaries gather information about their target to identify potential vulnerabilities and weaknesses. This phase can be further divided into two types: passive and active reconnaissance.

Passive Reconnaissance: Involves gathering information without directly interacting with the target. Attackers may use search engines, social media, and public databases to collect data about the organization, its employees, and its infrastructure.

Active Reconnaissance: Involves direct interaction with the target's systems, such as network scanning or probing web applications to identify live hosts, open ports, and services running.

Tactics and Techniques

- **Social Engineering**: Attackers may use social engineering tactics, such as pretexting or phishing, to trick employees into divulging sensitive information.
- **Network Scanning**: Tools like Nmap can be used to discover hosts and services on a network, allowing attackers to identify potential entry points.
- **Footprinting**: This involves creating a detailed map of the target's network and systems to understand its structure and vulnerabilities.

Defensive Measures

- **Security Awareness Training**: Educating employees about social engineering techniques can help prevent information leakage.
- **Network Monitoring**: Implementing intrusion detection systems (IDS) can help identify unusual scanning or probing activities.
- **Information Leakage Prevention**: Organizations should minimize the amount of sensitive information publicly available and regularly audit their online presence.

2. Scanning

Overview

In the scanning phase, attackers actively probe the target's systems to identify open ports, services, and potential vulnerabilities. This phase helps attackers refine their approach and focus on specific weaknesses.

Tactics and Techniques

- **Port Scanning**: Attackers use tools like Nmap to scan for open ports, which may indicate active services that could be exploited.

- **Service Enumeration**: After identifying open ports, attackers determine the services running on those ports to assess their security and identify known vulnerabilities.
- **Vulnerability Scanning**: Tools like Nessus or OpenVAS can be used to automate the detection of vulnerabilities in software and systems.

Defensive Measures

- **Network Segmentation**: Dividing the network into smaller segments can limit an attacker's ability to move laterally if they gain access.
- **Firewall Rules**: Implementing strict firewall rules can help control access to critical systems and reduce exposure to scanning.
- **Regular Vulnerability Assessments**: Conducting routine vulnerability scans can help organizations identify and remediate security weaknesses before they can be exploited.

3. Gaining Access

Overview

Once attackers have identified vulnerabilities, the next phase involves gaining unauthorized access to the target's systems. This phase often relies on the exploitation of known vulnerabilities, stolen credentials, or social engineering.

Tactics and Techniques

- **Exploitation of Vulnerabilities**: Attackers may use exploit kits or custom scripts to target specific vulnerabilities in software or systems.
- **Credential Dumping**: Tools like Mimikatz can extract credentials from memory, allowing attackers to gain access to accounts with elevated privileges.
- **Phishing Attacks**: Attackers may use phishing emails to trick users into providing their login credentials or downloading malware.

Defensive Measures

- **Patch Management**: Regularly updating software and systems can close vulnerabilities before they can be exploited.
- **Strong Authentication Practices**: Implementing multifactor authentication (MFA) can help protect accounts from unauthorized access.

- **Email Filtering Solutions**: Using advanced email filtering solutions can help detect and block phishing attempts before they reach users.

4. Maintaining Access

Overview

After successfully gaining access to a system, attackers often establish a foothold to maintain access for future operations. This phase may involve installing backdoors, creating new user accounts, or leveraging legitimate administrative tools.

Tactics and Techniques

- **Backdoors**: Attackers may install backdoor malware to facilitate remote access to compromised systems, allowing them to return at will.
- **Web Shells**: Uploading web shells to web servers provides attackers with a persistent method for executing commands and managing compromised environments.
- **Credential Persistence**: Attackers can create new user accounts with administrative privileges or modify existing accounts to ensure continued access.

Defensive Measures

- **Continuous Monitoring**: Implementing logging and monitoring solutions can help detect unusual activities and unauthorized changes to systems.
- **Account Management Policies**: Regularly reviewing user accounts and permissions can help identify and remove unauthorized accounts.
- **Endpoint Protection**: Deploying advanced endpoint protection solutions can help detect and remove backdoor malware and other persistent threats.

5. Execution

Overview

In the execution phase, attackers carry out their objectives, which may involve data theft, system disruption, or further infiltration into the network. This phase often encompasses multiple actions and can lead to severe consequences for the target organization.

Tactics and Techniques

- **Data Exfiltration**: Attackers may use various methods to exfiltrate sensitive data, including encrypted channels or physical media like USB drives.
- **Destructive Actions**: In some cases, attackers may deploy ransomware or wiper malware to disrupt operations or extort the organization.
- **Lateral Movement**: Attackers may move laterally within the network to compromise additional systems and expand their control over the environment.

Defensive Measures

- **Data Loss Prevention (DLP):** Implementing DLP solutions can help monitor and protect sensitive data from unauthorized access and exfiltration.
- **Incident Response Plans**: Developing and rehearsing incident response plans ensures that organizations can quickly react to and mitigate the impact of an attack.
- **Regular Security Audits**: Conducting regular security audits and penetration tests can help identify weaknesses and improve overall security posture.

Understanding the phases of a cyber attack, from reconnaissance to execution, is essential for organizations striving to enhance their cybersecurity defenses. By recognizing the tactics, techniques, and procedures employed by adversaries at each stage, organizations can develop targeted strategies to mitigate risks and respond effectively to potential threats.

A proactive approach to cybersecurity involves not only defending against known attack vectors but also anticipating emerging threats and continuously adapting security practices. By investing in employee training, implementing robust security measures, and fostering a culture of security awareness, organizations can strengthen their resilience against the ever-evolving landscape of cyber attacks.

3.2. Common Attack Vectors and Methods

In the realm of cybersecurity, understanding the common attack vectors and methods used by adversaries is vital for developing effective defense strategies. Attack vectors refer to the pathways or methods that cybercriminals utilize to gain unauthorized access to systems or networks. Each vector has its own set of tactics, techniques, and procedures (TTPs) that attackers employ to achieve their objectives. This chapter explores some of the most prevalent attack vectors and methods, providing insights into how they work and what organizations can do to defend against them.

1. Phishing

Overview

Phishing is one of the most common and effective attack vectors. It involves tricking individuals into revealing sensitive information, such as usernames, passwords, or financial information, by masquerading as a trustworthy entity in electronic communications.

Methods

- **Email Phishing**: Attackers send fraudulent emails that appear to come from legitimate organizations, often containing links to fake websites designed to steal credentials.
- **Spear Phishing**: A targeted form of phishing that focuses on specific individuals or organizations. Attackers often personalize the messages to increase the likelihood of success.
- **Whaling**: A type of spear phishing aimed at high-profile targets, such as executives or high-ranking officials, with the intent to extract sensitive information or money.

Defensive Measures

- **Security Awareness Training**: Regular training for employees on recognizing phishing attempts can significantly reduce the risk of successful attacks.
- **Email Filtering**: Implementing advanced email filtering solutions can help identify and block phishing emails before they reach users.
- **Multi-Factor Authentication (MFA):** Using MFA adds an additional layer of security, making it harder for attackers to gain access even if they have stolen credentials.

2. Malware

Overview

Malware, or malicious software, encompasses a wide range of harmful programs designed to infiltrate, damage, or gain unauthorized access to systems. This category includes viruses, worms, trojans, ransomware, and spyware.

Methods

- **Ransomware**: Malware that encrypts files on a victim's system and demands payment for the decryption key. Notable examples include WannaCry and Ryuk.
- **Trojans**: Malicious programs that disguise themselves as legitimate software to trick users into installing them. Once installed, they can steal data or create backdoors for attackers.
- **Keyloggers**: Software that records keystrokes to capture sensitive information like usernames and passwords.

Defensive Measures

- **Endpoint Protection**: Deploying robust endpoint protection solutions can help detect and eliminate malware threats before they can cause significant damage.
- **Regular Updates and Patching**: Keeping systems and software updated can close vulnerabilities that malware might exploit.
- **Backup Solutions**: Regularly backing up critical data can mitigate the impact of ransomware attacks, allowing organizations to restore data without paying the ransom.

3. Social Engineering

Overview

Social engineering exploits human psychology rather than technical vulnerabilities. Attackers manipulate individuals into divulging confidential information or performing actions that compromise security.

Methods

- **Pretexting**: The attacker creates a fabricated scenario to obtain sensitive information from the target. For example, pretending to be an IT support technician to gain access to a user's account.
- **Baiting**: Involves enticing victims to download malware or reveal information by offering something desirable, such as free software or media.
- **Tailgating**: An unauthorized individual gains physical access to a secure area by following someone who has legitimate access, often by pretending to be an employee.

Defensive Measures

- **Security Awareness Training**: Educating employees on social engineering tactics can empower them to recognize and resist manipulation attempts.
- **Access Controls**: Implementing strict access controls can limit the ability of unauthorized individuals to gain physical access to secure areas.
- **Incident Reporting Protocols**: Establishing clear protocols for reporting suspicious activities can help organizations quickly respond to potential security breaches.

4. SQL Injection

Overview

SQL injection is a web application vulnerability that allows attackers to interfere with the queries that an application makes to its database. By injecting malicious SQL code, attackers can manipulate databases to gain unauthorized access to data.

Methods

- **Exploitation**: Attackers craft input fields in web forms (e.g., login forms) to include malicious SQL statements, allowing them to retrieve sensitive information or modify database content.
- **Blind SQL Injection**: In scenarios where error messages are suppressed, attackers infer information about the database through systematic queries and observing application responses.

Defensive Measures

- **Input Validation**: Ensuring that user input is properly validated and sanitized can prevent SQL injection attacks from occurring.
- **Parameterized Queries**: Using prepared statements or parameterized queries can help separate SQL code from data, making it difficult for attackers to inject malicious code.
- **Regular Security Testing**: Conducting regular penetration tests and vulnerability assessments can help identify and remediate SQL injection vulnerabilities.

5. Distributed Denial of Service (DDoS)

Overview

A DDoS attack aims to overwhelm a target's systems, servers, or networks with a flood of internet traffic, rendering them unavailable to legitimate users. These attacks can cause significant downtime and financial losses.

Methods

- **Volume-Based Attacks**: Attackers use botnets to send massive amounts of traffic to a target, consuming bandwidth and resources.
- **Protocol Attacks**: These attacks exploit weaknesses in network protocols to disrupt services, such as SYN floods that consume server resources.
- **Application Layer Attacks**: Focus on specific applications, sending malicious requests to overwhelm the application's capabilities, often targeting web servers.

Defensive Measures

- **Traffic Analysis and Filtering**: Implementing traffic analysis tools can help identify and mitigate suspicious traffic patterns indicative of a DDoS attack.
- **Redundant Infrastructure**: Using load balancers and redundant servers can distribute traffic, reducing the impact of an attack.
- **DDoS Mitigation Services**: Organizations can leverage specialized DDoS mitigation services that absorb and mitigate attack traffic before it reaches their networks.

6. Credential Stuffing

Overview

Credential stuffing is an attack method that exploits users' tendency to reuse passwords across multiple sites. Attackers use lists of stolen credentials from one breach to gain unauthorized access to accounts on other platforms.

Methods

- **Automated Tools**: Attackers use automated tools to test large volumes of username-password combinations across various websites and services.
- **Botnets**: A botnet can be employed to distribute login attempts across different accounts and websites, making it harder for detection systems to respond.

Defensive Measures

- **Unique Password Policies**: Encouraging users to create unique passwords for each service can reduce the effectiveness of credential stuffing attacks.
- **Rate Limiting**: Implementing rate limiting can help slow down automated login attempts, making credential stuffing more difficult.
- **Monitoring for Unusual Activity**: Continuous monitoring of account logins can help detect and respond to suspicious login attempts quickly.

Understanding common attack vectors and methods is essential for organizations looking to bolster their cybersecurity defenses. By recognizing how attackers exploit vulnerabilities—whether through phishing, malware, social engineering, or more sophisticated techniques like SQL injection and DDoS attacks—organizations can better prepare themselves to prevent, detect, and respond to cyber threats.

Effective defense strategies must include a combination of technological solutions, employee training, and incident response planning. Cybersecurity is not solely about protecting systems; it's also about creating a culture of awareness and vigilance that can adapt to the ever-changing threat landscape. By continuously assessing risks and implementing robust security measures, organizations can enhance their resilience against the myriad of cyber threats they face today.

3.3. Post-Attack Impact and Recovery

The aftermath of a cyber attack can have profound implications for an organization, affecting its operations, reputation, and bottom line. Understanding the potential impacts of an attack and implementing an effective recovery strategy is crucial for minimizing damage and restoring normal operations. This chapter explores the various dimensions of post-attack impact, the recovery process, and best practices for organizations to enhance their resilience in the face of cyber threats.

1. Immediate Impact of a Cyber Attack

Operational Disruption

One of the most immediate effects of a cyber attack is the disruption of normal business operations. Systems may become inoperable, data may be lost or corrupted, and essential services can be interrupted, leading to significant downtime.

- **Loss of Access**: Attackers may deploy ransomware or other malicious software that locks users out of critical systems and data, halting operations.

- **System Performance Degradation**: Even after an attack, systems may operate at reduced capacity due to lingering malware or the need for extensive repairs.

Financial Costs

The financial implications of a cyber attack can be substantial and multi-faceted, encompassing immediate costs, regulatory fines, and long-term repercussions.

- **Direct Costs**: These include expenses related to incident response, system recovery, and potential ransom payments in the case of ransomware attacks.
- **Reputation Damage**: An organization's reputation can suffer considerably, impacting customer trust and leading to loss of business opportunities.

Data Loss and Theft

Cyber attacks often target sensitive data, which can be stolen, altered, or destroyed. The ramifications of data breaches can extend far beyond the immediate incident.

- **Loss of Intellectual Property**: Organizations may lose valuable intellectual property, affecting their competitive advantage.
- **Regulatory Compliance Issues**: Depending on the nature of the data lost, organizations may face legal ramifications, including fines for non-compliance with data protection regulations.

2. Recovery Process

The recovery process after a cyber attack involves several critical steps, each designed to restore operations and mitigate the impact of the incident.

Incident Response Team Activation

An effective incident response relies on a well-prepared team equipped to handle the aftermath of an attack. Key steps include:

- **Assessment of Damage**: The incident response team conducts an immediate assessment to determine the scope and impact of the attack, identifying affected systems and data.
- **Containment**: Measures are taken to contain the attack and prevent further damage, such as isolating affected systems or disabling compromised accounts.

Data Recovery and Restoration

Recovering lost or corrupted data is a crucial aspect of the recovery process. Strategies include:

- **Restoration from Backups**: Utilizing regular backups is essential for minimizing data loss. Organizations should have a robust backup strategy, ensuring that data can be quickly restored to a secure state.
- **Forensic Analysis**: Conducting a forensic analysis of affected systems can help identify the cause of the breach and assess the extent of data loss.

Communication and Reporting

Clear communication is vital during and after an attack. Organizations must:

- **Internal Communication**: Keep employees informed about the incident, outlining necessary actions and any changes in operations.
- **External Communication**: If sensitive customer data is involved, organizations must communicate transparently with affected stakeholders, adhering to legal and regulatory requirements.

3. Long-Term Impact and Strategic Recovery

The long-term impact of a cyber attack can influence an organization's strategic direction. Addressing these repercussions involves comprehensive planning and ongoing efforts to improve security posture.

Reviewing and Strengthening Security Posture

Post-attack evaluations often reveal vulnerabilities that need addressing. Organizations should:

- **Conduct Post-Mortem Analyses**: After recovery, it's crucial to analyze what went wrong and how to prevent similar incidents in the future. This may include revisiting security policies, procedures, and technologies.
- **Implement Enhanced Security Measures**: Organizations should invest in improved cybersecurity technologies, such as advanced threat detection systems and employee training programs, to enhance overall security.

Regaining Stakeholder Trust

Rebuilding trust after an attack is essential for maintaining customer relationships and reputation. Strategies include:

- **Transparency**: Openly sharing information about the attack, the response, and the measures taken to prevent future incidents can help restore stakeholder confidence.
- **Enhanced Customer Support**: Providing dedicated support to affected customers demonstrates commitment to their security and can mitigate reputational damage.

Compliance and Legal Considerations

Cyber attacks often have regulatory and legal implications that organizations must address post-incident.

- **Regulatory Reporting**: Depending on the nature of the breach, organizations may be required to notify regulatory bodies and affected individuals about the incident.
- **Legal Liability**: Engaging legal counsel can help navigate potential liabilities and understand the implications of the attack on ongoing operations.

4. Best Practices for Post-Attack Impact Mitigation

To effectively manage the impact of cyber attacks and enhance recovery efforts, organizations can adopt several best practices:

Develop and Regularly Update Incident Response Plans: Having a well-defined incident response plan can significantly improve the organization's ability to respond to and recover from an attack. Regular updates and drills help ensure that employees are familiar with the protocols.

Invest in Cybersecurity Insurance: Cyber insurance can help organizations mitigate financial losses resulting from a cyber attack, covering expenses related to incident response, legal fees, and regulatory fines.

Continuous Monitoring and Improvement: Organizations should engage in ongoing monitoring of their systems and threat landscape, adapting security measures as needed to protect against emerging threats.

Cultivate a Security-First Culture: Fostering a culture of security awareness and responsibility among employees can help reduce vulnerabilities and enhance the organization's overall resilience to attacks.

The post-attack impact and recovery process is a critical component of cybersecurity management. By understanding the immediate and long-term effects of a cyber attack, organizations can develop comprehensive strategies to mitigate damage and restore normal operations. Effective recovery involves a multi-faceted approach, combining incident response, data recovery, communication, and strategic improvements to security posture.

Ultimately, organizations must recognize that cybersecurity is an ongoing process, requiring continual adaptation to the evolving threat landscape. By prioritizing recovery efforts and implementing best practices, organizations can enhance their resilience, safeguard their assets, and maintain the trust of their stakeholders in an increasingly digital world.

4. Building a Red Team

Creating a successful red team is essential for organizations looking to bolster their cybersecurity defenses. A red team operates as an internal adversary, simulating real-world attacks to uncover vulnerabilities and strengthen an organization's security posture. However, assembling a high-performing red team requires more than just technical skills; it necessitates a diverse mix of expertise, creativity, and a collaborative mindset.

In this chapter, we will explore the critical elements involved in building an effective red team. We will discuss the essential skills and competencies needed, from technical proficiencies in penetration testing to soft skills such as communication and teamwork. Additionally, we will outline the various roles and responsibilities within a red team, emphasizing how each member contributes to the overall effectiveness of the team.

Moreover, we will delve into strategies for fostering a collaborative team culture, where innovation and learning thrive. By understanding the dynamics of a well-functioning red team, organizations can ensure that they are well-equipped to identify and mitigate vulnerabilities before they can be exploited by real adversaries. Join us as we lay the groundwork for building a formidable red team capable of adapting to the ever-changing cyber threat landscape.

4.1. Essential Skills and Competencies

Building an effective Red Team requires a diverse set of skills and competencies that empower team members to simulate real-world attacks, identify vulnerabilities, and ultimately strengthen an organization's cybersecurity posture. This chapter outlines the essential skills and competencies necessary for Red Team members, covering both technical and soft skills that contribute to the success of a Red Team operation.

1. Technical Skills

A. Penetration Testing and Ethical Hacking

At the core of Red Team operations is the ability to conduct penetration testing and ethical hacking. Team members must be proficient in:

- **Exploitation Techniques**: Understanding how to exploit vulnerabilities in various systems, applications, and networks. Familiarity with common tools and methodologies (e.g., OWASP Top Ten, Metasploit) is essential.
- **Network Protocols**: Knowledge of network protocols (TCP/IP, UDP, HTTP, DNS, etc.) and how they function allows team members to effectively navigate and manipulate network traffic.
- **Scripting and Programming**: Proficiency in scripting languages (e.g., Python, PowerShell, Bash) and programming languages (e.g., C, Java, JavaScript) enables team members to develop custom tools, automate tasks, and analyze vulnerabilities.

B. Vulnerability Assessment

A critical skill for Red Team members is the ability to assess and identify vulnerabilities within systems and applications. This includes:

- **Familiarity with Scanning Tools**: Using vulnerability scanners (e.g., Nessus, Qualys) to identify potential weaknesses and understand how to interpret the results.
- **Threat Modeling**: Understanding how to model potential threats and attack vectors specific to the organization's environment, enabling more focused assessments.

C. Exploit Development

The ability to develop and customize exploits is crucial for Red Team members aiming to bypass security controls. Key competencies include:

- **Understanding of Exploit Frameworks**: Familiarity with exploit development frameworks (e.g., Metasploit, Canvas) and how to modify existing exploits for specific targets.
- **Reverse Engineering**: Skills in reverse engineering binaries to understand how they work, identify vulnerabilities, and create custom exploits.

D. Security Controls and Mitigations

Knowledge of security controls and how to bypass them is essential for effective Red Team operations. This encompasses:

- **Understanding Security Technologies**: Familiarity with firewalls, intrusion detection systems (IDS), intrusion prevention systems (IPS), endpoint detection and response (EDR), and other security technologies helps Red Team members to design their attacks in ways that test these defenses.
- **Mitigation Techniques**: Knowing how to identify effective mitigation strategies that can be recommended to the Blue Team to enhance overall security.

2. Soft Skills

A. Communication

Effective communication is vital for Red Team members, both for internal collaboration and external reporting. Key aspects include:

- **Report Writing**: The ability to write clear and concise reports that document findings, methodologies, and recommendations. Reports should be tailored to various stakeholders, including technical teams and executive leadership.
- **Presentation Skills**: Being able to present findings and recommendations in a way that resonates with different audiences, facilitating understanding and encouraging action.

B. Team Collaboration

Red Team operations often involve collaboration with other team members and departments. Essential competencies include:

- **Interpersonal Skills**: Building relationships and working effectively with others is crucial, as Red Teams often collaborate with Blue Teams, IT departments, and management.
- **Adaptability**: The ability to adapt to changing situations and respond to unexpected challenges during engagements is essential for success.

C. Problem-Solving and Critical Thinking

Red Team members must possess strong problem-solving and critical-thinking skills, enabling them to devise creative solutions during engagements. This includes:

- **Analytical Thinking**: Evaluating complex situations, identifying patterns, and making informed decisions based on data and evidence.

- **Creative Approaches**: Developing innovative attack strategies and techniques that mimic real-world threat actors, keeping in mind that attackers often employ unique and unpredictable methods.

3. Knowledge of Cybersecurity Frameworks and Standards

A. Familiarity with Cybersecurity Frameworks

A strong understanding of cybersecurity frameworks (e.g., NIST, MITRE ATT&CK) and industry standards is essential for Red Team members. This knowledge helps inform their approaches to assessment and reporting. Key components include:

- **NIST Cybersecurity Framework**: Understanding the framework's core functions (Identify, Protect, Detect, Respond, Recover) can guide the Red Team in aligning their objectives with overall organizational security goals.
- **MITRE ATT&CK Framework**: Familiarity with this comprehensive knowledge base of adversary tactics, techniques, and procedures can help Red Team members simulate real-world attacks more effectively.

B. Regulatory Compliance Awareness

Red Team members should also have knowledge of relevant regulatory requirements (e.g., GDPR, HIPAA, PCI-DSS) to understand the compliance landscape in which organizations operate. This helps ensure that Red Team assessments align with legal and regulatory expectations.

4. Continuous Learning and Adaptability

A. Keeping Up with Evolving Threats

The cybersecurity landscape is constantly changing, with new threats and vulnerabilities emerging regularly. Red Team members must be committed to continuous learning, including:

- **Staying Updated on Threat Intelligence**: Regularly consuming threat intelligence reports, vulnerability databases (e.g., CVE, NVD), and security blogs to stay informed about the latest attack techniques and trends.
- **Participating in Training and Certifications**: Pursuing relevant certifications (e.g., OSCP, CEH, CISSP) and attending training sessions and conferences to enhance their skills and knowledge.

B. Flexibility in Approach

Given the dynamic nature of cyber threats, Red Team members must remain flexible and willing to adapt their methodologies based on new information and changing circumstances.

Building a successful Red Team requires a diverse mix of essential skills and competencies. Technical expertise in penetration testing, vulnerability assessment, and exploit development forms the foundation of Red Team operations. However, soft skills such as communication, teamwork, and critical thinking are equally important for ensuring that the team operates effectively and delivers meaningful insights to the organization.

Moreover, a solid understanding of cybersecurity frameworks and compliance requirements enhances the Red Team's ability to align its objectives with the organization's security goals. Continuous learning and adaptability are vital in keeping pace with the rapidly evolving threat landscape, allowing Red Team members to stay ahead of adversaries and effectively contribute to enhancing the organization's cybersecurity posture. By fostering these skills and competencies, organizations can build a Red Team capable of simulating realistic attacks and driving meaningful improvements in their overall security practices.

4.2. Team Roles and Responsibilities

A well-structured Red Team is essential for effectively simulating cyber attacks and identifying vulnerabilities within an organization's systems and processes. Each member plays a crucial role in the team's overall success, contributing unique skills and expertise to ensure comprehensive and realistic assessments. This chapter outlines the various roles and responsibilities within a Red Team, emphasizing how each position collaborates to achieve common goals.

1. Red Team Leader

Overview

The Red Team Leader is responsible for overseeing the entire Red Team operation, ensuring that all activities align with the organization's goals and objectives. This role requires a combination of technical knowledge, leadership skills, and strategic vision.

Key Responsibilities

- **Strategic Planning**: Develops and implements the Red Team's objectives, including engagement planning and scoping activities.
- **Team Coordination**: Coordinates team members, assigning roles and responsibilities based on individual strengths and expertise.
- **Stakeholder Communication**: Serves as the primary point of contact for senior management and other stakeholders, providing updates on engagements, findings, and recommendations.

2. Penetration Tester / Ethical Hacker

Overview

Penetration testers, also known as ethical hackers, are responsible for executing simulated attacks on the organization's systems, applications, and networks to identify vulnerabilities and weaknesses.

Key Responsibilities

- **Engagement Execution**: Conducts penetration tests using a variety of methodologies, tools, and techniques to simulate real-world attacks.
- **Vulnerability Discovery**: Identifies and exploits vulnerabilities in applications and systems, documenting the findings for later analysis.
- **Reporting Findings**: Prepares detailed reports outlining the vulnerabilities discovered, the methods used to exploit them, and recommendations for remediation.

3. Threat Intelligence Analyst

Overview

The Threat Intelligence Analyst focuses on understanding the threat landscape and identifying potential adversaries, their tactics, techniques, and procedures (TTPs). This role is crucial for informing Red Team engagements and ensuring they align with real-world threats.

Key Responsibilities

- **Threat Research**: Conducts research on emerging threats, vulnerabilities, and trends in the cybersecurity landscape.
- **TTP Analysis**: Analyzes and documents the TTPs used by known adversaries to inform the Red Team's attack strategies.
- **Engagement Preparation**: Collaborates with the Red Team to develop scenarios and attack vectors based on threat intelligence.

4. Social Engineer

Overview

The Social Engineer specializes in employing social engineering techniques to simulate human vulnerabilities within an organization. This role focuses on understanding and exploiting human behavior to gain access to sensitive information or systems.

Key Responsibilities

- **Phishing Campaigns**: Designs and executes phishing simulations to test employee awareness and response to social engineering attacks.
- **Physical Security Assessments**: Conducts assessments of physical security by attempting to gain unauthorized access to facilities through techniques such as tailgating or pretexting.
- **Reporting and Recommendations**: Provides feedback to the organization on employee susceptibility to social engineering attacks and recommends training to improve awareness.

5. Malware Analyst

Overview

The Malware Analyst specializes in the analysis and development of malware used in Red Team operations. This role focuses on understanding how malware operates and how to deploy it effectively during engagements.

Key Responsibilities

- **Malware Development**: Creates custom malware to simulate advanced persistent threats (APTs) and test defenses against sophisticated attacks.
- **Malware Analysis**: Analyzes existing malware samples to understand their behavior and identify potential detection evasion techniques.

- **Tool Development**: Develops tools to assist the Red Team in executing engagements and avoiding detection by security systems.

6. Systems Administrator

Overview

The Systems Administrator plays a critical role in managing and maintaining the technical infrastructure needed for Red Team operations. This role ensures that the tools and systems used during engagements are configured correctly and function as intended.

Key Responsibilities

- **Environment Setup**: Prepares and configures environments, including virtual machines and cloud resources, for Red Team engagements.
- **Tool Maintenance**: Maintains and updates the tools and software used by the Red Team, ensuring they are effective and up to date.
- **System Monitoring**: Monitors systems for anomalies during engagements and ensures that security measures are in place to protect sensitive data.

7. Red Team Analyst

Overview

The Red Team Analyst supports the overall operation by analyzing data collected during engagements, identifying trends, and assisting in reporting findings.

Key Responsibilities

- **Data Analysis**: Reviews logs, attack vectors, and outcomes from Red Team engagements to identify patterns and areas for improvement.
- **Documentation**: Assists in the documentation of findings, creating detailed reports for both technical and non-technical audiences.
- **Feedback and Improvement**: Provides feedback on Red Team processes and suggests improvements based on engagement outcomes.

8. Blue Team Liaison

Overview

The Blue Team Liaison acts as a bridge between the Red Team and the Blue Team (defensive security team), ensuring that insights gained during Red Team engagements are communicated effectively and lead to improvements in defensive measures.

Key Responsibilities

- **Collaboration**: Works closely with the Blue Team to share findings, attack simulations, and recommendations for improving security posture.
- **Knowledge Transfer**: Facilitates training sessions for Blue Team members to enhance their understanding of Red Team methodologies and improve their defenses.
- **Continuous Improvement**: Collaborates on developing proactive measures based on insights gained from Red Team operations, fostering a culture of continuous improvement.

A successful Red Team relies on the collaboration of diverse roles, each contributing essential skills and expertise to the overall mission. From leadership and strategic planning to technical execution and analysis, every member plays a vital part in identifying vulnerabilities and improving an organization's cybersecurity posture.

Understanding the specific roles and responsibilities within the Red Team not only enhances operational effectiveness but also promotes collaboration and knowledge sharing. By fostering a culture of teamwork and continuous improvement, organizations can leverage the full potential of their Red Team to simulate realistic attacks, strengthen defenses, and ultimately build a more resilient cyber landscape.

4.3. Cultivating a Collaborative Team Culture

A successful Red Team operates within a culture of collaboration, trust, and shared purpose. The effectiveness of Red Team operations is often determined not just by the technical skills of its members, but by the team's ability to work together cohesively toward common objectives. This chapter explores the principles and practices necessary to cultivate a collaborative team culture within a Red Team, emphasizing the importance of communication, trust-building, and continuous improvement.

1. Establishing Clear Communication

A. Open Lines of Communication

Effective communication is the backbone of collaboration within a Red Team. Establishing open lines of communication ensures that team members can share ideas, insights, and feedback freely. Key practices include:

- **Regular Meetings**: Scheduling regular check-ins and team meetings encourages members to discuss ongoing projects, share updates, and address challenges collectively.
- **Collaboration Tools**: Utilizing collaboration tools (e.g., Slack, Microsoft Teams, JIRA) enhances communication, allowing team members to share information in real time and collaborate on projects seamlessly.

B. Active Listening

Encouraging active listening among team members fosters an environment where everyone feels valued and heard. This involves:

- **Encouraging Participation**: Creating a safe space for team members to express their opinions and ideas without fear of judgment.
- **Acknowledging Contributions**: Recognizing and appreciating the input and expertise of each team member reinforces their sense of belonging and encourages further participation.

2. Building Trust and Respect

A. Trust-Building Activities

Trust is essential for effective collaboration. Engaging in trust-building activities can strengthen relationships within the team. Activities may include:

- **Team-Building Exercises**: Participating in team-building exercises, such as escape rooms or problem-solving challenges, helps build camaraderie and trust among members.
- **Social Interactions**: Encouraging informal gatherings, such as team lunches or outings, allows team members to connect on a personal level, fostering deeper relationships.

B. Respect for Expertise

Recognizing and respecting the diverse expertise within the team is crucial. This includes:

- **Role Acknowledgment**: Understanding and appreciating the unique skills and contributions of each team member promotes mutual respect and collaboration.
- **Encouraging Knowledge Sharing**: Creating opportunities for team members to share their expertise through presentations, workshops, or knowledge-sharing sessions fosters a culture of learning.

3. Encouraging Collaborative Problem-Solving

A. Collective Brainstorming Sessions

Facilitating collective brainstorming sessions encourages team members to work together to solve complex problems and develop creative solutions. This involves:

- **Structured Sessions**: Organizing structured brainstorming sessions where team members can propose ideas and build on each other's suggestions.
- **Diverse Perspectives**: Inviting input from all team members ensures that diverse perspectives are considered, leading to more innovative and effective solutions.

B. Pairing and Mentorship

Encouraging pairing and mentorship within the team fosters collaboration and knowledge transfer. This can include:

- **Pair Programming**: Pairing team members with different skills or experience levels during technical tasks promotes learning and collaboration.
- **Mentorship Programs**: Establishing mentorship programs allows experienced members to guide and support newer team members, fostering a sense of belonging and encouraging professional growth.

4. Embracing a Culture of Continuous Improvement

A. Feedback Loops

Establishing a culture of continuous improvement involves creating feedback loops that allow team members to learn from each engagement. This can include:

- **Post-Engagement Debriefs**: Conducting debrief sessions after Red Team engagements to discuss what went well, what didn't, and how the team can improve in future operations.

- **Constructive Feedback**: Encouraging team members to provide constructive feedback to one another fosters a culture of learning and growth.

B. Celebrating Achievements

Recognizing and celebrating the team's achievements, both big and small, reinforces a sense of accomplishment and motivation. This can include:

- **Recognition Programs**: Implementing recognition programs or awards for outstanding contributions fosters a positive team culture and encourages continued excellence.
- **Sharing Success Stories**: Highlighting successful engagements and the positive impact of the Red Team's work helps build pride in the team's accomplishments.

5. Fostering Inclusivity and Diversity

A. Embracing Diverse Perspectives

A collaborative team culture thrives on inclusivity and diversity. Embracing diverse perspectives can enhance problem-solving and innovation. This involves:

- **Diverse Recruitment**: Actively seeking diverse candidates during recruitment to ensure a wide range of perspectives and experiences within the team.
- **Inclusive Environment**: Creating an inclusive environment where all team members feel valued and empowered to contribute, regardless of their background.

B. Addressing Challenges

Addressing challenges related to inclusivity and diversity is crucial for maintaining a collaborative culture. This includes:

- **Awareness Training**: Providing training on unconscious bias and inclusivity to promote awareness and understanding among team members.
- **Encouraging Open Dialogue**: Facilitating open discussions about diversity and inclusion allows team members to share their experiences and perspectives, fostering a supportive environment.

Cultivating a collaborative team culture within a Red Team is essential for achieving successful outcomes and enhancing the overall effectiveness of cybersecurity efforts. By establishing clear communication, building trust and respect, encouraging collaborative problem-solving, embracing continuous improvement, and fostering inclusivity, organizations can create an environment where team members feel empowered and motivated to excel.

A collaborative culture not only enhances the performance of the Red Team but also contributes to the broader cybersecurity landscape, as insights gained from Red Team engagements can drive improvements in defensive measures and strengthen the organization's overall security posture. As the threat landscape continues to evolve, the importance of collaboration and teamwork in addressing these challenges cannot be overstated. By fostering a culture of collaboration, organizations can better prepare for and respond to the complexities of modern cybersecurity threats.

5. Planning and Scoping Red Team Engagements

Effective red team engagements are rooted in careful planning and precise scoping. Without a clear framework, these simulations can lead to misaligned objectives, unanticipated risks, and ultimately, missed opportunities for improvement. Proper planning not only ensures that the red team operates within defined parameters but also maximizes the value of the engagement for the organization.

In this chapter, we will explore the key elements involved in planning and scoping red team engagements. We will discuss how to define clear objectives that align with the organization's security goals and business needs. Establishing boundaries is crucial, as it helps protect sensitive systems and data while ensuring compliance with legal and ethical standards.

We will also delve into the importance of stakeholder communication, emphasizing the need for buy-in from key decision-makers and the integration of insights from blue teams. By fostering collaboration and transparency, organizations can create a more effective environment for red team operations.

Through real-world examples and best practices, this chapter will equip you with the knowledge and tools necessary to plan and scope red team engagements effectively. With a solid foundation in place, you can enhance the overall impact of your red teaming efforts and drive meaningful improvements in your organization's cybersecurity posture.

5.1. Defining Objectives and Success Criteria

Defining clear objectives and success criteria is a critical step in the planning and scoping phase of Red Team engagements. This ensures that both the Red Team and stakeholders have a shared understanding of the goals of the engagement and how success will be measured. This chapter delves into the importance of setting objectives, outlining practical steps for defining them, and establishing criteria for evaluating the success of Red Team operations.

1. Importance of Clear Objectives

A. Alignment with Organizational Goals

Establishing clear objectives ensures that Red Team engagements align with the broader goals of the organization. This alignment is essential for several reasons:

- **Strategic Relevance**: Clear objectives help ensure that the Red Team's activities address the organization's most pressing security concerns, such as critical assets, compliance requirements, or emerging threats.
- **Resource Allocation**: Defining objectives allows organizations to allocate resources more effectively, ensuring that time, budget, and personnel are directed toward high-priority areas.

B. Guiding Engagement Scope and Methodology

Objectives serve as a roadmap for how the Red Team will approach the engagement. They guide decisions regarding:

- **Scope Definition**: Objectives help determine the scope of the engagement, including which systems, applications, or processes will be tested and the methods that will be employed.
- **Engagement Methodology**: A clear understanding of the objectives influences the choice of methodologies, attack vectors, and tools used during the engagement.

2. Steps for Defining Objectives

A. Engage Stakeholders

Collaborating with stakeholders from various departments (e.g., IT, compliance, risk management) is essential for defining relevant and meaningful objectives. Steps include:

- **Identify Key Stakeholders**: Determine who will be impacted by the Red Team engagement, including senior management, security teams, and operational staff.
- **Gather Input**: Conduct interviews or workshops to gather insights on the organization's security priorities, concerns, and objectives.

B. Prioritize Objectives

After gathering input from stakeholders, it's important to prioritize the objectives based on their significance to the organization. This can involve:

- **Risk Assessment**: Assessing the risks associated with different systems, applications, and processes to determine which areas require the most attention.
- **Feasibility Considerations**: Evaluating the feasibility of each objective based on resource availability, time constraints, and technical capabilities.

C. Formulate SMART Objectives

Using the SMART criteria (Specific, Measurable, Achievable, Relevant, Time-bound) can help ensure that objectives are well-defined. Examples include:

- **Specific**: "Test the security of the corporate intranet application to identify potential vulnerabilities."
- **Measurable**: "Identify at least five vulnerabilities in the application and provide remediation recommendations."
- **Achievable**: Ensure that the objectives are realistic given the team's resources and capabilities.
- **Relevant**: Align the objectives with the organization's overall security goals and priorities.
- **Time-bound**: Set a clear timeline for the engagement, such as "Complete the assessment within four weeks."

3. Establishing Success Criteria

A. Defining Metrics for Success

Once objectives are established, it's crucial to define metrics that will be used to evaluate the success of the engagement. Key metrics may include:

- **Number of Vulnerabilities Identified**: Quantifying the vulnerabilities discovered during the engagement provides a concrete measure of success.
- **Severity of Vulnerabilities**: Categorizing vulnerabilities based on severity (e.g., critical, high, medium, low) to assess the overall impact of the findings.
- **Remediation Recommendations**: Evaluating the quality and effectiveness of the remediation recommendations provided to stakeholders.

B. Stakeholder Feedback

Gathering feedback from stakeholders post-engagement is an essential component of evaluating success. This can involve:

- **Surveys and Interviews**: Conducting surveys or interviews with stakeholders to assess their satisfaction with the engagement, the quality of findings, and the utility of recommendations.
- **Follow-up Meetings**: Holding follow-up meetings to discuss feedback, address concerns, and identify areas for improvement in future engagements.

4. Documenting Objectives and Success Criteria

A. Engagement Planning Document

Creating a comprehensive engagement planning document that outlines the defined objectives and success criteria is crucial for ensuring clarity and alignment. This document should include:

- **Engagement Overview**: A summary of the engagement's purpose, scope, and methodology.
- **Objectives List**: A detailed list of objectives that the Red Team aims to achieve during the engagement.
- **Success Criteria**: Clearly defined metrics and criteria for evaluating the success of the engagement.

B. Communication with Stakeholders

Effectively communicating the objectives and success criteria to stakeholders helps ensure that everyone is on the same page. This includes:

- **Presentation**: Presenting the engagement planning document to stakeholders for review and approval.
- **Ongoing Updates**: Keeping stakeholders informed of progress throughout the engagement, reinforcing the shared objectives and expectations.

Defining clear objectives and success criteria is a foundational step in the planning and scoping of Red Team engagements. By engaging stakeholders, formulating SMART objectives, and establishing metrics for success, organizations can ensure that their Red Team activities align with strategic priorities and effectively address critical security concerns.

A well-defined engagement not only guides the Red Team's efforts but also enhances accountability and transparency, ensuring that stakeholders understand the purpose and value of the engagement. As a result, organizations can leverage Red Team operations to drive meaningful improvements in their overall security posture and resilience against evolving cyber threats.

5.2. Establishing Engagement Boundaries

Establishing clear engagement boundaries is a crucial aspect of planning Red Team operations. Boundaries define the limits within which the Red Team can operate, ensuring that the engagement remains focused, controlled, and compliant with organizational policies and legal requirements. This chapter explores the importance of defining engagement boundaries, key considerations in the process, and best practices for ensuring that Red Team operations remain effective while minimizing risks.

1. Importance of Defining Engagement Boundaries

A. Protecting Organizational Assets

Engagement boundaries serve to protect the organization's critical assets, systems, and data during Red Team operations. Clear boundaries help ensure that:

- **Critical Systems Remain Operational**: By defining which systems and applications are in-scope and out-of-scope, organizations can ensure that essential operations are not disrupted during testing.
- **Sensitive Data is Secured**: Clearly established boundaries prevent unauthorized access to sensitive data, maintaining compliance with data protection regulations and safeguarding the organization's reputation.

B. Legal and Compliance Considerations

Defining engagement boundaries is also vital for ensuring compliance with legal and regulatory requirements. This involves:

- **Avoiding Legal Liability**: Clearly delineating the scope of the engagement helps avoid potential legal ramifications associated with unauthorized access to systems or data.
- **Adhering to Regulations**: Compliance with industry regulations (such as GDPR, HIPAA, PCI-DSS) requires careful consideration of what data and systems can be tested and how.

2. Key Considerations for Establishing Boundaries

A. Scope of the Engagement

The scope of the engagement outlines the specific systems, applications, and processes that the Red Team will assess. Key considerations include:

- **In-Scope Systems**: Clearly identify which systems and applications are included in the testing. This may involve web applications, internal networks, cloud services, and other digital assets.
- **Out-of-Scope Systems**: Define which systems and applications are explicitly excluded from testing to avoid any potential disruption or unintended consequences.

B. Engagement Duration

Establishing the timeline for the engagement helps set expectations and ensures that both the Red Team and stakeholders understand the timeframe for testing. This includes:

- **Testing Phases**: Defining different phases of the engagement (e.g., reconnaissance, exploitation, reporting) and their respective durations.
- **Flexibility**: Allowing for some flexibility in the timeline to accommodate unexpected challenges or findings, while still adhering to the overall schedule.

C. Types of Testing Allowed

Clearly specifying the types of testing permitted during the engagement is essential to maintain control and compliance. This includes:

- **Allowed Techniques**: Defining the methodologies and techniques the Red Team is authorized to use, such as social engineering, phishing, or network penetration testing.
- **Prohibited Activities**: Explicitly stating any activities that are off-limits (e.g., denial-of-service attacks, physical security breaches) to prevent unintentional damage or disruption.

3. Best Practices for Establishing Engagement Boundaries

A. Collaborate with Stakeholders

Engaging stakeholders from various departments (e.g., IT, legal, compliance) in the boundary-setting process is essential for ensuring comprehensive understanding and agreement. This involves:

- **Cross-Functional Meetings**: Organizing meetings with key stakeholders to discuss the scope and boundaries of the engagement, addressing concerns and gathering input.
- **Formal Approval**: Obtaining formal approval from stakeholders, ensuring that everyone is on board with the defined boundaries and understands their implications.

B. Document Boundaries Clearly

Creating a formal document that outlines the engagement boundaries provides a reference for the Red Team and stakeholders. This document should include:

- **Engagement Overview**: A brief description of the engagement, its objectives, and relevance to organizational goals.
- **Defined Boundaries**: A detailed section specifying in-scope and out-of-scope systems, testing types, and any legal considerations.

C. Communication of Boundaries

Effective communication of established boundaries to all team members is crucial for ensuring adherence during the engagement. This includes:

- **Pre-Engagement Briefings**: Conducting briefings with the Red Team to review the boundaries and expectations before testing begins.
- **Ongoing Reminders**: Providing regular reminders of the boundaries throughout the engagement to maintain focus and adherence.

4. Monitoring and Adjusting Boundaries During Engagements

A. Continuous Oversight

Maintaining oversight during the engagement helps ensure that boundaries are respected and that the team is adhering to the established protocols. This involves:

- **Real-Time Monitoring**: Utilizing monitoring tools and dashboards to observe the engagement in real time, ensuring compliance with the defined boundaries.

- **Regular Check-Ins**: Scheduling regular check-ins with the Red Team to discuss progress and address any concerns or potential boundary violations.

B. Flexibility to Adjust

While boundaries provide structure, there may be instances where adjustments are necessary based on findings or changing circumstances. This includes:

- **Re-Evaluating Boundaries**: Periodically reassessing the boundaries during the engagement based on discoveries or unforeseen challenges, with input from stakeholders.
- **Communicating Changes**: Clearly communicating any adjustments to the Red Team and stakeholders to ensure everyone remains informed and aligned.

Establishing clear engagement boundaries is essential for ensuring that Red Team operations are effective, safe, and compliant with organizational policies and legal requirements. By defining the scope of testing, engagement duration, and allowed techniques, organizations can protect critical assets and maintain operational integrity.

Engaging stakeholders in the boundary-setting process, documenting boundaries clearly, and maintaining effective communication throughout the engagement are best practices that enhance the effectiveness of Red Team operations. Furthermore, continuous oversight and the flexibility to adjust boundaries as needed contribute to a successful engagement that yields valuable insights while minimizing risks. By adhering to these principles, organizations can leverage Red Team engagements to strengthen their cybersecurity posture while fostering a culture of collaboration and compliance.

5.3. Stakeholder Communication and Buy-in

Effective communication and buy-in from stakeholders are critical components of successful Red Team engagements. Gaining the support of key stakeholders ensures that the objectives of the Red Team are aligned with organizational priorities, and that the engagement is conducted smoothly and effectively. This chapter explores strategies for effective stakeholder communication, the importance of buy-in, and best practices for fostering collaboration and support throughout the engagement process.

1. Importance of Stakeholder Communication

A. Aligning Objectives and Expectations

Clear communication with stakeholders helps align the objectives of the Red Team engagement with the broader goals of the organization. This alignment is essential for:

- **Strategic Relevance**: Ensuring that the Red Team's activities address the organization's most pressing security concerns and priorities.
- **Resource Allocation**: Facilitating effective resource allocation by clearly articulating the expected outcomes and benefits of the engagement to stakeholders.

B. Building Trust and Confidence

Open and transparent communication fosters trust between the Red Team and stakeholders. This trust is vital for:

- **Support During Engagement**: Gaining stakeholder support for any necessary disruptions or changes in operations during the engagement.
- **Post-Engagement Follow-Up**: Enhancing stakeholder confidence in the Red Team's findings and recommendations, leading to better acceptance of proposed remediation actions.

2. Identifying Key Stakeholders

A. Mapping Stakeholder Landscape

Identifying and mapping the key stakeholders involved in or impacted by the Red Team engagement is the first step in effective communication. This involves:

- **Stakeholder Categories**: Categorizing stakeholders into groups, such as executive leadership, IT security teams, risk management, compliance officers, and operational staff.
- **Understanding Roles**: Recognizing the roles and responsibilities of each stakeholder group in relation to the Red Team engagement and its outcomes.

B. Prioritizing Stakeholder Engagement

Not all stakeholders are equally impacted by the Red Team's activities. Prioritizing engagement based on influence and impact helps focus communication efforts. This can involve:

- **Influence Matrix**: Creating an influence matrix to assess stakeholders based on their level of influence and interest in the engagement.
- **Tailored Communication Plans**: Developing tailored communication plans for high-priority stakeholders to ensure their specific concerns and interests are addressed.

3. Developing a Communication Strategy

A. Defining Communication Goals

Establishing clear communication goals is crucial for ensuring effective stakeholder engagement. Key goals may include:

- **Informing Stakeholders**: Providing stakeholders with relevant information about the objectives, scope, and expected outcomes of the engagement.
- **Gathering Feedback**: Encouraging input from stakeholders to ensure their concerns and perspectives are considered in the planning process.

B. Choosing Communication Channels

Selecting the right communication channels is essential for effective stakeholder engagement. This may involve:

- **Formal Presentations**: Conducting formal presentations or briefings to introduce the Red Team engagement to stakeholders, outlining objectives and expected outcomes.
- **Informal Meetings**: Organizing informal meetings or roundtable discussions to facilitate open dialogue and gather feedback from stakeholders.

C. Establishing a Communication Schedule

Creating a communication schedule helps ensure timely updates and information sharing throughout the engagement. This includes:

- **Regular Updates**: Scheduling regular updates (weekly or bi-weekly) to keep stakeholders informed about progress and any significant findings.
- **Milestone Communications**: Planning communications around key milestones, such as the completion of phases or delivery of initial findings.

4. Strategies for Gaining Stakeholder Buy-In

A. Highlighting Value and Benefits

To gain stakeholder buy-in, it is essential to clearly articulate the value and benefits of the Red Team engagement. This involves:

- **Risk Reduction**: Emphasizing how the engagement will help identify vulnerabilities and reduce risk to the organization's critical assets.
- **Compliance and Regulatory Alignment**: Highlighting the engagement's role in ensuring compliance with industry regulations and standards.

B. Engaging Stakeholders Early

Involving stakeholders early in the engagement process fosters a sense of ownership and investment in the outcomes. This can include:

- **Initial Briefings**: Conducting initial briefings to introduce stakeholders to the Red Team's objectives and methodologies.
- **Feedback Sessions**: Holding feedback sessions to gather input on the proposed objectives and scope, ensuring stakeholder perspectives are considered.

C. Addressing Concerns and Misconceptions

Anticipating and addressing potential concerns or misconceptions about the Red Team engagement is crucial for gaining buy-in. This may involve:

- **Clarifying Roles**: Clearly communicating the roles of the Red Team and stakeholders during the engagement, dispelling any fears of intrusion or disruption.
- **Explaining Methodologies**: Providing insights into the methodologies and tools used by the Red Team, reassuring stakeholders that testing will be conducted responsibly and ethically.

5. Maintaining Ongoing Communication

A. Regular Check-Ins During the Engagement

Maintaining ongoing communication with stakeholders throughout the engagement is vital for keeping them informed and engaged. This can involve:

- **Progress Reports**: Providing regular progress reports that highlight key findings, ongoing activities, and any emerging issues.
- **Advisory Meetings**: Organizing advisory meetings to discuss findings, address concerns, and gather stakeholder input on next steps.

B. Post-Engagement Review and Feedback

After the engagement concludes, conducting a post-engagement review with stakeholders helps solidify buy-in and encourages future collaboration. This involves:

- **Presentation of Findings**: Presenting the final findings and recommendations in a clear and accessible manner, ensuring stakeholders understand the implications.
- **Feedback Collection**: Gathering feedback on the engagement process and outcomes to identify areas for improvement in future engagements.

Effective stakeholder communication and buy-in are essential for the success of Red Team engagements. By clearly articulating objectives, engaging stakeholders early, and maintaining ongoing communication throughout the engagement process, organizations can foster trust and collaboration.

Establishing a comprehensive communication strategy that identifies key stakeholders, defines communication goals, and highlights the value of the engagement ensures that all parties are aligned and invested in the outcomes. By addressing concerns and misconceptions, and maintaining open lines of communication, organizations can enhance the effectiveness of their Red Team operations, driving meaningful improvements in their overall cybersecurity posture. Ultimately, fostering a culture of collaboration and support contributes to a more resilient organization, better prepared to face the evolving threat landscape.

6. Tools of the Trade

In the realm of red teaming, having the right tools at your disposal can make all the difference between a successful engagement and a missed opportunity to uncover vulnerabilities. The landscape of cybersecurity is rich with a diverse array of tools designed to assist red teamers in executing their strategies effectively, ranging from automated scanning solutions to sophisticated exploitation frameworks.

In this chapter, we will explore the essential tools and technologies that form the backbone of a red team's arsenal. We will categorize these tools based on their primary functions, including reconnaissance, vulnerability assessment, exploitation, and post-exploitation analysis. Understanding the strengths and limitations of each tool will empower red teamers to select the most appropriate resources for their specific objectives.

Additionally, we will discuss the importance of automation and scripting in streamlining red team operations, enabling teams to conduct efficient and thorough assessments. The integration of various tools into a cohesive workflow is essential for maximizing effectiveness and minimizing operational overhead.

By examining real-world applications and case studies, this chapter will provide you with insights into how to effectively leverage these tools in your own red teaming efforts. As we navigate through the various resources available, you'll gain a clearer understanding of how to enhance your skills and optimize your engagements in the pursuit of robust cybersecurity.

6.1. Essential Red Teaming Tools and Software

In the ever-evolving landscape of cybersecurity, Red Team engagements require a suite of specialized tools and software to effectively simulate real-world attacks and identify vulnerabilities within an organization's infrastructure. This chapter explores the essential tools and software utilized by Red Teams, categorizing them based on their primary functions, and providing insights into how these tools contribute to successful engagements.

1. Overview of Red Teaming Tools

Red Teaming tools can be broadly categorized into several categories based on their functionality, including reconnaissance, exploitation, post-exploitation, and reporting.

Each category serves a specific purpose in the Red Team engagement process, facilitating a comprehensive assessment of the organization's security posture.

2. Categories of Red Teaming Tools

A. Reconnaissance Tools

Reconnaissance is the initial phase of a Red Team engagement, where the team gathers information about the target organization. Effective reconnaissance tools help identify assets, network infrastructure, and potential vulnerabilities. Key tools in this category include:

Nmap: A widely used network scanning tool that allows Red Teams to discover hosts and services on a network, identify open ports, and gather information about the target system.

Maltego: An advanced data mining tool that helps visualize relationships between various entities, such as people, organizations, and infrastructure. Maltego is particularly useful for social engineering attacks and mapping out the target environment.

Recon-ng: A web reconnaissance framework that provides a powerful environment for gathering open-source intelligence (OSINT). It includes modules for data collection, analysis, and reporting, making it a versatile tool for initial reconnaissance.

B. Exploitation Tools

Once potential vulnerabilities are identified, exploitation tools are used to gain unauthorized access or control over systems. These tools enable Red Teams to simulate real-world attacks effectively. Notable exploitation tools include:

Metasploit Framework: A comprehensive penetration testing framework that provides a wide array of exploits, payloads, and auxiliary modules. Metasploit allows Red Teams to automate the exploitation process and test various attack vectors efficiently.

Burp Suite: A popular tool for web application security testing, Burp Suite includes features for scanning, crawling, and attacking web applications. Its interactive nature allows Red Teams to manipulate requests and responses in real time.

SQLMap: An automated tool for detecting and exploiting SQL injection vulnerabilities. SQLMap simplifies the process of testing web applications for database vulnerabilities and can be highly effective in gaining access to sensitive information.

C. Post-Exploitation Tools

After successfully exploiting a system, Red Teams must assess the impact and maintain access. Post-exploitation tools help with lateral movement, privilege escalation, and data exfiltration. Key tools in this category include:

Empire: A post-exploitation framework that allows Red Teams to execute PowerShell agents for command and control. Empire provides a wide range of modules for lateral movement, credential harvesting, and persistence.

Cobalt Strike: A commercial penetration testing tool that provides a robust platform for simulating advanced threat actors. Cobalt Strike includes features for social engineering, lateral movement, and command-and-control communications.

Mimikatz: A tool for extracting plaintext passwords, hash credentials, and Kerberos tickets from memory. Mimikatz is invaluable for credential harvesting during post-exploitation phases.

D. Reporting and Collaboration Tools

Documentation and reporting are essential components of the Red Team engagement process. Effective reporting tools ensure that findings are communicated clearly and actionable recommendations are provided. Key tools in this category include:

Dradis: An open-source reporting tool that allows Red Teams to document findings, collaborate on assessments, and generate professional reports. Dradis helps streamline the documentation process and enhance communication within the team.

Faraday: An integrated multi-user platform for vulnerability management and collaboration. Faraday supports various penetration testing tools and allows teams to share findings in real time, facilitating effective collaboration.

ReportGenerator: A tool designed to automate the generation of HTML reports from various security tools' output. ReportGenerator helps Red Teams consolidate findings and present them in a user-friendly format.

3. Best Practices for Tool Selection

A. Evaluate Organizational Needs

When selecting tools for Red Team engagements, organizations should assess their specific needs and objectives. This involves:

- **Understanding Engagement Goals**: Clearly defining the objectives of the Red Team engagement to identify which tools will best support those goals.
- **Assessing Existing Infrastructure**: Evaluating the organization's existing security infrastructure and tools to determine compatibility and integration opportunities.

B. Consider Tool Usability and Community Support

The usability of tools and the level of community support can significantly impact their effectiveness. Organizations should consider:

- **User-Friendly Interfaces**: Choosing tools with intuitive interfaces that facilitate efficient use and minimize the learning curve for team members.
- **Active Community and Documentation**: Selecting tools with strong community support and comprehensive documentation to ensure access to resources, tutorials, and updates.

C. Stay Updated with Emerging Tools

The cybersecurity landscape is continuously evolving, and new tools are regularly developed to address emerging threats. Red Teams should:

- **Regularly Review Tools**: Conduct periodic reviews of the tools used in engagements to identify new solutions that could enhance capabilities and improve efficiency.
- **Participate in Community Discussions**: Engage with the cybersecurity community through forums, conferences, and social media to stay informed about the latest trends and tools in the industry.

The effectiveness of Red Team engagements heavily relies on the tools and software utilized throughout the process. By leveraging essential tools for reconnaissance, exploitation, post-exploitation, and reporting, Red Teams can conduct comprehensive assessments that simulate real-world attack scenarios.

Selecting the right tools involves evaluating organizational needs, considering usability, and staying updated with emerging solutions. By following best practices for tool selection and remaining adaptable to the evolving threat landscape, Red Teams can enhance their capabilities, ultimately contributing to a more resilient cybersecurity posture for the organizations they serve. Through strategic use of these tools, Red Teams can uncover vulnerabilities, recommend effective remediation strategies, and strengthen the overall security framework of the organization.

6.2. Automation and Scripting Techniques

In the fast-paced world of cybersecurity, efficiency and speed are paramount, especially during Red Team engagements. Automation and scripting techniques play a crucial role in enhancing the capabilities of Red Teams, allowing them to conduct assessments more thoroughly and quickly while minimizing human error. This chapter delves into the importance of automation in Red Teaming, explores various scripting techniques, and highlights popular tools and languages used for automation in cybersecurity.

1. Importance of Automation in Red Teaming

A. Increased Efficiency

Automation allows Red Teams to streamline repetitive tasks, significantly reducing the time and effort required for certain activities. This leads to:

- **Faster Reconnaissance**: Automated tools can quickly gather information about a target, such as open ports, running services, and exposed assets, allowing the team to focus on analysis rather than data collection.
- **Consistent Testing**: Automated scripts ensure that testing methodologies are applied consistently across different engagements, reducing variability in results.

B. Enhanced Coverage

Automation enables Red Teams to cover a broader attack surface more effectively. By using scripts and automated tools, teams can:

- **Conduct Comprehensive Scans**: Automated tools can scan large networks or web applications, identifying vulnerabilities that might be overlooked in manual testing.

- **Execute Multiple Attack Scenarios**: Automation allows for the simultaneous execution of various attack vectors, increasing the likelihood of uncovering potential weaknesses.

C. Reducing Human Error

Automating certain processes helps minimize the risk of human error, which can lead to overlooked vulnerabilities or incorrect configurations. By relying on tested scripts and tools, Red Teams can ensure:

- **Accuracy in Testing**: Automated tools consistently perform actions according to predefined parameters, reducing the likelihood of mistakes that can occur in manual testing.
- **Reproducibility**: Automated processes can be replicated easily across different environments or engagements, ensuring that findings are reliable and comparable.

2. Scripting Techniques in Red Teaming

A. Common Scripting Languages

Red Teams often utilize various programming and scripting languages to automate tasks and create custom tools. Some of the most common languages include:

Python: Widely used in cybersecurity due to its versatility and extensive libraries, Python can automate tasks like web scraping, API interaction, and network scanning. Libraries such as requests, Beautiful Soup, and Scapy are particularly useful for Red Teaming.

PowerShell: A powerful scripting language native to Windows environments, PowerShell is commonly used for automating administrative tasks, conducting reconnaissance, and executing post-exploitation techniques. Its deep integration with the Windows operating system allows for effective system manipulation and management.

Bash: The default shell scripting language for Unix-based systems, Bash scripts are useful for automating tasks in Linux environments, such as scanning, data collection, and reporting.

B. Common Automation Techniques

Several automation techniques are employed by Red Teams to enhance their efficiency and effectiveness during engagements:

Automated Reconnaissance: Using scripts to automate the collection of information about a target, including DNS queries, IP address lookups, and port scanning. Tools like Amass and Nmap can be integrated into automated workflows to streamline reconnaissance.

Vulnerability Scanning: Automating vulnerability scanning processes with tools like Nessus, OpenVAS, or Qualys. Scripts can be created to schedule scans, gather results, and analyze vulnerabilities across systems.

Payload Delivery: Automating the delivery of malicious payloads during exploitation phases. This can include using frameworks like Metasploit to create and deploy payloads programmatically.

Data Exfiltration: Automating the process of extracting sensitive data from compromised systems. This may involve writing scripts that leverage protocols like FTP, HTTP, or custom APIs for data transfer.

3. Popular Automation Tools

A. Metasploit Framework

Metasploit is one of the most popular penetration testing frameworks that support automation. It allows Red Teams to:

- **Automate Exploitation**: Use built-in modules to automate various exploitation techniques and deploy payloads efficiently.
- **Scripted Attacks**: Integrate Metasploit with Ruby scripts to create custom workflows that automate attack chains.

B. BloodHound

BloodHound is a tool used to analyze Active Directory environments. It helps Red Teams visualize relationships and permissions within AD and can be automated to:

- **Gather Information**: Use automated scripts to collect data about users, groups, and permissions.
- **Generate Reports**: Produce visualizations and reports on the AD structure to identify potential attack paths.

C. Cobalt Strike

Cobalt Strike is a commercial tool designed for advanced threat emulation. It allows for automation through:

- **Aggressor Script**: A built-in scripting language that allows users to automate tasks within Cobalt Strike, such as deploying payloads or interacting with compromised systems.
- **Beacon Automation**: Using Cobalt Strike's Beacon functionality to automate command-and-control (C2) interactions during engagements.

4. Best Practices for Automation and Scripting

A. Maintain Clarity and Documentation

As Red Teams develop scripts and automated processes, it is crucial to maintain clarity and thorough documentation. This includes:

- **Commenting Code**: Writing clear comments within scripts to explain functionality and logic, making it easier for team members to understand and modify the code.
- **Version Control**: Utilizing version control systems like Git to track changes and collaborate effectively on scripts and automation tools.

B. Test Scripts Thoroughly

Before deploying scripts in a live engagement, thorough testing is essential to ensure they work as intended. This includes:

- **Testing in Isolated Environments**: Running scripts in a controlled environment to validate functionality and identify potential issues without impacting production systems.
- **Simulating Real-World Scenarios**: Testing scripts against realistic scenarios to ensure they perform as expected during engagements.

C. Incorporate Feedback Loops

Implementing feedback loops allows Red Teams to refine their automation processes continuously. This involves:

- **Reviewing Outcomes**: Analyzing the results of automated tasks and identifying areas for improvement.
- **Iterating on Scripts**: Updating and optimizing scripts based on feedback from team members and the outcomes of previous engagements.

Automation and scripting techniques are integral to the effectiveness of Red Team engagements. By leveraging a variety of scripting languages and automation tools, Red Teams can enhance their efficiency, coverage, and accuracy during assessments.

With a focus on clear documentation, thorough testing, and continuous improvement, organizations can optimize their automation efforts, ultimately leading to more effective identification of vulnerabilities and strengthening of cybersecurity defenses. As the threat landscape continues to evolve, the role of automation in Red Teaming will only grow in importance, enabling teams to stay ahead of adversaries and effectively safeguard their organizations.

6.3. Evaluating Tool Effectiveness and Integration

As organizations invest in Red Teaming capabilities, the selection and integration of the right tools are essential to achieving successful outcomes. Evaluating tool effectiveness and ensuring seamless integration with existing systems can enhance operational efficiency and ultimately strengthen an organization's cybersecurity posture. This chapter outlines the key criteria for assessing the effectiveness of Red Teaming tools, explores the importance of integration, and provides best practices for achieving both.

1. Evaluating Tool Effectiveness

A. Criteria for Assessment

When evaluating Red Teaming tools, organizations should consider several key criteria to determine their effectiveness:

Functionality: Does the tool meet the specific needs of the Red Team? This includes assessing whether it can perform the required tasks, such as reconnaissance, exploitation, or post-exploitation. Tools should align with the objectives of the Red Team engagement.

Usability: How user-friendly is the tool? A tool with a steep learning curve can hinder productivity. The interface should be intuitive, and comprehensive documentation or support should be available to assist users.

Performance: How well does the tool perform in real-world scenarios? This involves assessing its speed, reliability, and accuracy. Performance testing can be conducted in controlled environments to ensure the tool operates effectively under various conditions.

Scalability: Can the tool scale to meet the needs of the organization? As Red Teams often work on diverse engagements, a tool should be capable of handling varying network sizes, complexities, and threat scenarios.

Community Support and Updates: Does the tool have an active community or vendor support? Frequent updates and an engaged user community can enhance the tool's effectiveness by addressing vulnerabilities, adding features, and providing ongoing support.

B. Conducting a Tool Evaluation Process

To systematically evaluate Red Teaming tools, organizations can follow a structured process:

Define Objectives: Establish clear objectives for the evaluation process based on the organization's specific needs and goals for Red Team engagements.

Create a Testing Environment: Set up a controlled environment where tools can be tested without impacting production systems. This environment should mimic the target systems and configurations.

Test Scenarios: Develop test scenarios that reflect real-world attack vectors and challenges. These scenarios should cover various functionalities of the tools being evaluated.

Gather Feedback: Involve Red Team members in the evaluation process and collect their feedback on the tool's performance, usability, and effectiveness in completing assigned tasks.

Analyze Results: After testing, analyze the results to determine which tools met the established criteria and identify any gaps or areas for improvement.

Document Findings: Maintain thorough documentation of the evaluation process, including performance metrics, feedback, and final recommendations for tool selection.

2. Integration of Tools into Existing Workflows

A. Importance of Integration

Effective integration of Red Teaming tools into existing workflows is vital for maximizing their value. This involves:

Seamless Collaboration: Integrated tools enable better collaboration among team members, allowing them to share information, findings, and processes more effectively.

Enhanced Data Flow: Integrating tools allows for smoother data flow between systems, reducing manual entry and the potential for errors. This can streamline the reporting process and facilitate quicker decision-making.

Consistent Methodologies: Integration promotes the use of consistent methodologies across different engagements, ensuring that tools are utilized in a standard manner and that findings are comparable.

B. Strategies for Effective Integration

To successfully integrate Red Teaming tools into existing workflows, organizations can employ the following strategies:

Assess Existing Infrastructure: Evaluate the current cybersecurity tools and platforms in use to identify opportunities for integration. This includes understanding how new tools will interact with existing systems.

Establish Integration Points: Identify specific integration points where tools can share data or communicate with one another. This may involve leveraging APIs, webhooks, or custom scripts to facilitate data exchange.

Develop Workflows: Create standardized workflows that incorporate the use of Red Teaming tools. This includes outlining how tools will be used in different phases of an engagement, from reconnaissance to reporting.

Training and Documentation: Provide training for team members on how to effectively use and integrate the tools into their workflows. Comprehensive documentation should be maintained to guide users in the integration process.

Continuous Improvement: Regularly assess the effectiveness of tool integration and make adjustments as needed. This includes gathering feedback from users and monitoring the performance of integrated tools during engagements.

3. Measuring Success and Performance

A. Key Performance Indicators (KPIs)

To evaluate the success of tool effectiveness and integration, organizations should establish key performance indicators (KPIs) that align with their Red Team objectives:

Engagement Efficiency: Measure the time taken to complete various phases of Red Team engagements before and after tool integration. A reduction in time indicates improved efficiency.

Vulnerability Identification Rates: Track the number of vulnerabilities identified during engagements using the integrated tools. An increase in identified vulnerabilities can demonstrate the effectiveness of the tools.

Team Productivity: Assess the productivity of Red Team members by evaluating the number of engagements completed and the quality of findings reported. Enhanced productivity may reflect the successful integration of tools.

Stakeholder Satisfaction: Gather feedback from stakeholders on the quality of reports and recommendations produced as a result of Red Team engagements. Higher satisfaction levels indicate effective tool utilization and integration.

B. Continuous Monitoring and Feedback

Establish a process for continuous monitoring of tool effectiveness and integration performance. This involves:

Regular Reviews: Schedule periodic reviews to evaluate the performance of Red Teaming tools and their integration within workflows. These reviews should include assessments of user feedback and engagement outcomes.

Adaptation and Upgrades: Stay informed about updates to tools and emerging technologies that could enhance Red Team capabilities. Be prepared to adapt tools and workflows based on lessons learned and new developments in the field.

Fostering a Feedback Culture: Encourage an open feedback culture where team members can share their experiences and suggestions for improving tool effectiveness and integration. This collaborative approach can lead to ongoing enhancements.

Evaluating the effectiveness of Red Teaming tools and ensuring their seamless integration into existing workflows are critical components of a successful Red Team operation. By systematically assessing tools based on established criteria and fostering collaboration through integration, organizations can enhance their Red Team capabilities and improve their overall cybersecurity posture.

The ongoing evaluation and adaptation of tools and processes allow Red Teams to remain agile and responsive to the ever-changing threat landscape. Ultimately, the combination of effective tool utilization and integration contributes to a more robust and resilient security environment, enabling organizations to proactively identify and address vulnerabilities before they can be exploited by adversaries.

7. Executing Realistic Attack Scenarios

The effectiveness of a red team largely hinges on its ability to simulate realistic attack scenarios that mirror the tactics used by actual adversaries. By creating scenarios that reflect the evolving threat landscape, red teams can uncover vulnerabilities and weaknesses in an organization's defenses, providing invaluable insights that drive meaningful improvements.

In this chapter, we will explore the critical steps involved in designing and executing realistic attack scenarios. We will discuss the importance of threat modeling and intelligence gathering to ensure that your simulations are not only plausible but also relevant to your organization's unique risk profile. Understanding the motivations and methods of potential adversaries is key to crafting scenarios that challenge existing security measures.

We will also delve into various attack types, including social engineering, phishing, and physical security assessments, examining how each can be effectively executed within the context of a red team engagement. Practical examples will illustrate how to balance creativity and realism in your scenarios, ensuring they provide a comprehensive test of the organization's security posture.

As we navigate the complexities of executing realistic attack scenarios, you will gain the insights needed to elevate your red teaming efforts, ultimately fostering a more resilient cybersecurity framework capable of withstanding real-world threats.

7.1. Designing Simulated Attack Scenarios

Simulated attack scenarios form the backbone of Red Team operations, enabling cybersecurity professionals to evaluate the effectiveness of an organization's defenses and identify potential vulnerabilities. By meticulously crafting realistic scenarios that mimic real-world attack techniques, Red Teams can provide invaluable insights into the resilience of an organization's security posture. This chapter explores the essential elements involved in designing effective simulated attack scenarios, methodologies for scenario creation, and the importance of aligning these scenarios with the organization's specific threat landscape.

1. Understanding the Purpose of Simulated Attack Scenarios

A. Assessing Security Posture

The primary objective of simulated attack scenarios is to assess the current security posture of an organization. This includes:

Identifying Vulnerabilities: By replicating specific attack vectors, Red Teams can uncover weaknesses in systems, applications, and processes that may be exploited by real-world adversaries.

Testing Incident Response: Simulated attacks provide a controlled environment for evaluating how effectively the organization can respond to security incidents. This helps in identifying gaps in incident response plans and improving overall preparedness.

B. Enhancing Security Awareness

Simulated attack scenarios also serve to increase security awareness within the organization. Through realistic simulations, employees can:

Understand Threats: Employees gain a better understanding of the tactics, techniques, and procedures (TTPs) used by attackers, helping to foster a security-conscious culture.

Practice Responses: Employees can practice their responses to simulated attacks, ensuring they are better prepared to handle actual incidents.

2. Key Elements of Effective Attack Scenarios

A. Realism and Relevance

To ensure the effectiveness of simulated attack scenarios, they must be realistic and relevant to the organization's environment. This involves:

Contextualization: Scenarios should be based on the specific technologies, assets, and processes present in the organization. This increases the likelihood of identifying relevant vulnerabilities and weaknesses.

Adversarial Realism: Scenarios should incorporate realistic attacker profiles, motivations, and tactics. Understanding the adversary's goals and methods helps in designing scenarios that accurately reflect potential threats.

B. Scope and Complexity

Determining the scope and complexity of an attack scenario is crucial. This involves:

Defining Engagement Boundaries: Clearly outlining the boundaries of the engagement, including which systems and data are in scope, helps to manage risks and ensures compliance with legal and organizational policies.

Balancing Complexity: Scenarios should strike a balance between complexity and feasibility. While complex scenarios may offer deeper insights, they should remain achievable within the time and resource constraints of the engagement.

C. Objectives and Success Criteria

Each simulated attack scenario should have clear objectives and success criteria. This includes:

Defining Goals: Establishing specific goals for the simulation, such as testing a particular attack vector, assessing the effectiveness of security controls, or evaluating incident response capabilities.

Success Metrics: Identifying measurable success criteria helps determine the effectiveness of the scenario. This may include metrics such as the number of vulnerabilities identified, the time taken to detect the attack, or the effectiveness of incident response measures.

3. Methodologies for Scenario Design

A. Threat Modeling

Threat modeling is a systematic approach to identifying and prioritizing potential threats. It involves:

Asset Identification: Identifying critical assets within the organization, such as sensitive data, critical infrastructure, and key applications.

Identifying Threat Actors: Understanding potential adversaries, their motivations, capabilities, and the methods they may employ to target the organization.

Mapping Attack Vectors: Analyzing how adversaries could exploit vulnerabilities to achieve their goals, and developing scenarios that reflect these attack paths.

B. Scenario Frameworks

Utilizing established frameworks can help structure the design process. Some popular frameworks include:

MITRE ATT&CK: This framework provides a comprehensive matrix of known adversarial tactics and techniques. Red Teams can use it to select specific TTPs for inclusion in their scenarios, ensuring alignment with real-world attack methods.

Cyber Kill Chain: Developed by Lockheed Martin, the Cyber Kill Chain outlines the stages of a cyber attack, from reconnaissance to exploitation and beyond. Red Teams can design scenarios that reflect different stages of the kill chain, allowing for a holistic assessment of security defenses.

NIST SP 800-115: This guide outlines technical aspects of conducting penetration testing. It provides a structured approach to designing and executing simulated attack scenarios, emphasizing the importance of defining clear objectives and deliverables.

C. Collaborative Design

Involving stakeholders from various departments can enhance the quality and relevance of simulated attack scenarios. This includes:

Interdisciplinary Collaboration: Engaging representatives from IT, security, and operational teams fosters a holistic understanding of the organization's systems and processes, allowing for more effective scenario design.

Feedback and Iteration: After initial design drafts, gathering feedback from stakeholders can identify potential blind spots or areas for improvement. Iterative design processes ensure that scenarios remain aligned with organizational needs and risks.

4. Documenting and Communicating Scenarios

A. Scenario Documentation

Thorough documentation of each simulated attack scenario is essential for clarity and consistency. Documentation should include:

Scenario Description: A detailed narrative of the attack scenario, including objectives, expected outcomes, and any relevant background information.

Step-by-Step Execution Plan: A clear outline of the steps to be taken during the simulation, including any tools or techniques that will be utilized.

Success Criteria: Specific metrics or indicators that will be used to evaluate the success of the scenario upon completion.

B. Communication with Stakeholders

Effective communication with stakeholders is crucial for ensuring buy-in and understanding of the simulated attack scenarios. This involves:

Pre-Engagement Briefings: Conducting briefings before the engagement to inform relevant stakeholders about the planned scenarios, objectives, and any potential impacts on operations.

Post-Engagement Reporting: After the simulation, providing comprehensive reports to stakeholders detailing findings, insights, and recommendations for improvement.

Designing simulated attack scenarios is a critical aspect of Red Team operations, enabling organizations to assess their cybersecurity defenses and enhance their incident response capabilities. By ensuring scenarios are realistic, relevant, and aligned with organizational objectives, Red Teams can uncover vulnerabilities and provide valuable insights for improving security posture.

Utilizing structured methodologies, involving stakeholders, and maintaining clear documentation are essential components of effective scenario design. As organizations face an ever-evolving threat landscape, the ability to simulate realistic attacks will continue to play a vital role in strengthening cybersecurity defenses and fostering a culture of security awareness. By proactively identifying weaknesses and enhancing preparedness, organizations can better defend against real-world adversaries and safeguard their critical assets.

7.2. Conducting Social Engineering Tests

Social engineering tests are essential components of a comprehensive Red Teaming strategy, designed to assess an organization's susceptibility to human manipulation.

Unlike traditional technical attacks, social engineering exploits human psychology, targeting the vulnerabilities of individuals rather than systems. This chapter explores the principles behind social engineering, the methodologies for conducting tests, and the importance of ethical considerations in ensuring the integrity and effectiveness of these engagements.

1. Understanding Social Engineering

A. Definition and Purpose

Social engineering refers to the psychological manipulation of individuals to perform actions or divulge confidential information. In the context of cybersecurity, social engineering tests aim to:

Evaluate Security Awareness: Assess how well employees recognize and respond to social engineering attempts, thereby identifying weaknesses in the organization's security culture.

Uncover Vulnerabilities: Highlight areas where employees may inadvertently expose the organization to risk, such as revealing sensitive information or providing unauthorized access.

B. Types of Social Engineering Attacks

Understanding the different types of social engineering attacks helps Red Teams design effective tests. Common types include:

Phishing: Deceptive emails or messages that trick users into providing sensitive information or downloading malware.

Pretexting: Creating a fabricated scenario to obtain information, often by impersonating a trusted authority or colleague.

Baiting: Offering something enticing, such as free software or rewards, to encourage users to disclose information or download malicious content.

Tailgating: Gaining unauthorized access to a restricted area by following someone who has legitimate access, often by pretending to be an employee.

2. Planning and Designing Social Engineering Tests

A. Setting Objectives

Before conducting social engineering tests, it's crucial to establish clear objectives that align with the organization's overall security goals. Common objectives include:

Measuring Employee Awareness: Assessing how well employees recognize and respond to social engineering attempts.

Identifying Weak Points: Discovering specific departments or roles that may be more vulnerable to manipulation.

Testing Response Protocols: Evaluating how effectively employees report suspicious activity or incidents.

B. Crafting Realistic Scenarios

To ensure the effectiveness of social engineering tests, scenarios should be carefully crafted to reflect real-world attack vectors. This involves:

Researching the Target Environment: Gathering information about the organization, its employees, and its operations to create realistic scenarios. This includes understanding company hierarchy, communication styles, and potential vulnerabilities.

Creating Pretexts: Developing credible personas and narratives that will resonate with employees. For instance, impersonating a technical support staff member or a vendor can increase the likelihood of success.

Choosing Appropriate Channels: Selecting the most effective channels for conducting the test, whether through email, phone calls, or in-person interactions.

3. Executing Social Engineering Tests

A. Test Execution

The execution phase is where the planned social engineering tests are carried out. Key considerations include:

Maintaining Professionalism: Conducting tests in a manner that reflects professionalism and minimizes disruption to daily operations. It's essential to maintain a respectful approach to avoid damaging trust within the organization.

Monitoring Responses: Observing how employees respond to the social engineering attempts. This may involve tracking interactions, noting the time taken to respond, and recording any information disclosed.

Documenting Findings: Keeping detailed records of the test outcomes, including successful and unsuccessful attempts. This documentation will be critical for analysis and reporting later.

B. Adapting in Real Time

During the execution of social engineering tests, Red Team members should be prepared to adapt their approach based on employee responses. This may involve:

Altering Tactics: If an initial approach fails, testers may need to pivot to a different strategy or persona that may resonate more effectively with employees.

Using Humor and Rapport: Building rapport and using light humor can sometimes disarm employees and facilitate the conversation, increasing the likelihood of success.

4. Analyzing Results and Reporting

A. Evaluating Test Outcomes

After conducting social engineering tests, it's essential to analyze the results to gain insights into employee behavior and organizational vulnerabilities. Key areas of focus include:

Success Rates: Calculating the percentage of employees who fell for the social engineering attempts, which can highlight the overall vulnerability of the organization.

Types of Information Disclosed: Reviewing what information employees disclosed can help identify specific areas of risk and the effectiveness of current training programs.

Response Time and Behavior: Assessing how quickly and effectively employees reported suspicious activity can provide insights into the organization's incident response culture.

B. Reporting Findings

Comprehensive reporting is critical for translating test results into actionable insights. Effective reports should include:

Executive Summary: A high-level overview of the test objectives, methodologies, and key findings, tailored for stakeholders.

Detailed Findings: A breakdown of each social engineering attempt, including successful and unsuccessful scenarios, along with an analysis of employee responses.

Recommendations for Improvement: Providing practical recommendations for enhancing security awareness, including potential training programs and policy updates.

5. Ethical Considerations

A. Ethical Implications

Conducting social engineering tests raises ethical considerations that must be carefully managed. Red Teams should adhere to the following principles:

Informed Consent: Ensure that the organization is aware of the nature of the tests being conducted, and obtain necessary approvals from management.

Minimizing Disruption: Conduct tests in a manner that minimizes disruption to normal business operations and maintains employee trust.

Protecting Privacy: Safeguard employee privacy by avoiding the collection of sensitive personal information during tests.

B. Debriefing Employees

After completing social engineering tests, it's essential to debrief employees who participated in the scenarios. This includes:

Providing Feedback: Offering constructive feedback to employees about their responses, emphasizing positive actions and areas for improvement.

Educating on Risks: Using the debriefing as an opportunity to educate employees about social engineering tactics, empowering them to recognize and respond to real threats in the future.

Conducting social engineering tests is a critical component of Red Team operations, enabling organizations to evaluate their vulnerabilities and enhance their security awareness. By carefully planning and executing realistic tests, Red Teams can provide valuable insights into employee behavior and organizational resilience.

Ethical considerations must guide the process, ensuring that tests are conducted with respect and transparency. The lessons learned from social engineering tests can inform training programs, incident response protocols, and organizational policies, ultimately fostering a culture of security awareness and resilience. In a landscape where human factors play a significant role in cybersecurity, understanding and mitigating social engineering risks is essential for safeguarding an organization's assets and reputation.

7.3. Engaging in Physical Security Assessments

Physical security assessments are a vital component of a comprehensive Red Teaming strategy. While much attention in cybersecurity focuses on digital threats, physical vulnerabilities can also pose significant risks to an organization's assets, personnel, and information. This chapter explores the process of conducting physical security assessments, the methodologies used, and the critical importance of integrating physical and cybersecurity efforts to create a robust security posture.

1. Understanding the Importance of Physical Security Assessments

A. Definition of Physical Security

Physical security refers to the protective measures that an organization employs to safeguard its physical assets from unauthorized access, damage, theft, or natural disasters. These measures can include physical barriers, surveillance systems, access control protocols, and environmental controls.

B. Why Physical Security Matters

Physical security is essential for several reasons:

Protection of Sensitive Information: Many organizations store sensitive data in physical form, such as documents or hardware. Ensuring physical security helps protect this information from theft or unauthorized access.

Safeguarding Employees: Effective physical security measures protect employees from potential threats, including violence, theft, and other risks.

Preventing Damage to Infrastructure: Physical security measures help prevent damage to critical infrastructure and systems, which can lead to significant financial and operational impacts.

Compliance Requirements: Many industries have regulations that mandate specific physical security measures to protect sensitive information, such as healthcare or financial sectors.

2. Planning and Preparing for Physical Security Assessments

A. Defining Objectives

Before initiating a physical security assessment, it's crucial to define clear objectives that align with the organization's overall security goals. Common objectives include:

Identifying Vulnerabilities: Assessing the effectiveness of existing physical security measures and identifying areas of weakness that could be exploited by unauthorized individuals.

Testing Incident Response Protocols: Evaluating how effectively the organization's personnel respond to potential breaches or threats to physical security.

Enhancing Security Awareness: Increasing employee awareness of physical security risks and promoting a culture of vigilance.

B. Gathering Background Information

Effective planning involves gathering background information about the organization, including:

Site Layout: Understanding the layout of facilities, including entrances, exits, sensitive areas, and security infrastructure.

Existing Security Measures: Reviewing current physical security measures, such as access control systems, surveillance cameras, and security personnel presence.

Historical Security Incidents: Analyzing past security incidents to identify patterns or recurring vulnerabilities that need addressing.

3. Conducting the Physical Security Assessment

A. Site Walkthrough

The assessment begins with a comprehensive walkthrough of the facility, which involves:

Observational Assessment: Evaluating physical security measures in place, such as locks, barriers, lighting, and signage. Observers should note any areas that appear vulnerable or inadequately secured.

Testing Access Controls: Assessing the effectiveness of access control measures by attempting to gain unauthorized entry to restricted areas or observing how access is granted.

Reviewing Security Protocols: Observing how security personnel interact with employees and visitors, and assessing whether established protocols are being followed consistently.

B. Social Engineering Techniques

Red Teams can incorporate social engineering techniques into physical security assessments to evaluate employee awareness and adherence to security policies. This may include:

Tailgating Tests: Attempting to gain access to restricted areas by following authorized personnel without their knowledge. This helps assess the vigilance of employees in recognizing and responding to potential threats.

Pretexting for Access: Utilizing pretexts (such as pretending to be a maintenance worker or delivery person) to gauge how easily employees will grant access to restricted areas.

Unauthorized Photography or Observation: Trying to discreetly observe sensitive areas or documents to evaluate how well employees protect confidential information.

4. Analyzing Findings and Reporting

A. Documenting Observations

Throughout the assessment, detailed notes and observations should be documented, including:

Identified Vulnerabilities: A comprehensive list of vulnerabilities observed during the assessment, categorized by severity and potential impact.

Employee Behavior: Notes on employee responses to social engineering attempts, including successes and failures, and general awareness of physical security practices.

Compliance with Policies: Evaluating whether employees followed established security policies and protocols.

B. Reporting Results

After the assessment, it's critical to compile a detailed report that includes:

Executive Summary: A high-level overview of the assessment, including key findings and recommendations, tailored for stakeholders.

Detailed Findings: A breakdown of observed vulnerabilities, employee behaviors, and any areas where physical security measures were insufficient.

Actionable Recommendations: Practical suggestions for enhancing physical security, including upgrades to infrastructure, employee training programs, and policy improvements.

5. Ethical Considerations

A. Ethical Implications of Physical Security Testing

Conducting physical security assessments raises ethical considerations that must be carefully managed. Key principles include:

Informed Consent: Ensure that organizational leadership is aware of the assessment scope and objectives, obtaining necessary approvals before conducting tests.

Minimizing Disruption: Conduct assessments in a manner that minimizes disruption to normal business operations and maintains employee trust.

Confidentiality: Protect sensitive information encountered during the assessment and ensure that findings are communicated only to authorized personnel.

B. Debriefing Employees

After completing the physical security assessment, it's important to debrief employees who participated in the tests. This involves:

Providing Feedback: Offering constructive feedback to employees about their responses to social engineering attempts and security protocols.

Training and Awareness: Using the debriefing as an opportunity to reinforce physical security policies and promote awareness of potential threats.

Engaging in physical security assessments is a critical aspect of Red Team operations that complements digital security efforts. By evaluating physical vulnerabilities and the effectiveness of existing security measures, organizations can better protect their assets, personnel, and information.

Through careful planning, execution, and analysis of physical security assessments, Red Teams can provide valuable insights into areas that need improvement. By addressing physical vulnerabilities and promoting a culture of security awareness, organizations can enhance their overall security posture and reduce the risks associated with unauthorized access and other physical threats. In an increasingly interconnected world, the integration of physical and cybersecurity measures is essential for safeguarding an organization's critical assets and ensuring its long-term resilience.

8. The Importance of Intelligence Gathering

In the world of cybersecurity, knowledge is power. Effective intelligence gathering serves as the foundation for successful red teaming, providing the insights necessary to anticipate, understand, and exploit vulnerabilities within an organization's defenses. By leveraging a variety of intelligence sources, red teams can craft more precise and impactful attack scenarios that mirror real-world threats.

In this chapter, we will explore the critical role of intelligence gathering in the red teaming process. We will begin by discussing the different types of intelligence—ranging from open-source intelligence (OSINT) to technical and human intelligence—and their relevance in shaping your red team strategy. Understanding how to collect and analyze this information is essential for creating attack scenarios that accurately reflect the tactics of actual adversaries.

We will also delve into the methodologies and tools available for effective reconnaissance, examining how to conduct thorough assessments of the target environment. By uncovering publicly available information and assessing the target's digital footprint, red teams can identify potential weaknesses before engaging in simulated attacks.

Through real-world examples and best practices, this chapter will equip you with the skills and techniques needed to enhance your intelligence gathering efforts. By integrating robust intelligence practices into your red teaming approach, you will improve your ability to anticipate threats and strengthen your organization's overall cybersecurity posture.

8.1. Open Source Intelligence (OSINT) Techniques

Open Source Intelligence (OSINT) is a crucial component of cybersecurity, providing organizations with the means to gather actionable information from publicly available sources. In the context of Red Team operations, OSINT techniques are employed to identify vulnerabilities, understand the threat landscape, and inform attack simulations. This chapter delves into the fundamental OSINT techniques, tools, and best practices that Red Teams can leverage to enhance their intelligence-gathering efforts.

1. Understanding Open Source Intelligence (OSINT)

A. Definition of OSINT

Open Source Intelligence (OSINT) refers to the process of collecting and analyzing information from publicly available sources to support decision-making. Unlike traditional intelligence, which may rely on classified or proprietary information, OSINT utilizes data from:

- Social media platforms
- Public records
- News articles and blogs
- Online forums and communities
- Company websites and press releases
- Academic papers and reports

B. Importance of OSINT in Red Teaming

OSINT plays a pivotal role in Red Team operations for several reasons:

Threat Landscape Awareness: OSINT helps Red Teams stay informed about current threats, vulnerabilities, and attack vectors that may affect their target organizations.

Identifying Attack Surfaces: By gathering information about an organization's infrastructure, systems, and personnel, Red Teams can identify potential attack surfaces for their engagements.

Enhancing Engagement Planning: OSINT provides valuable context for planning Red Team engagements, allowing for more realistic and effective attack simulations.

2. OSINT Techniques for Information Gathering

A. Search Engines and Advanced Queries

Search engines are powerful tools for gathering OSINT. Red Team members can utilize advanced search queries to uncover specific information, including:

Google Dorking: This technique involves using advanced search operators to find specific information or vulnerabilities. Examples include:

- **site**:example.com filetype:pdf to locate PDF documents on a specific domain.
- **inurl**:admin to find administrative login pages.

Specialized Search Engines: In addition to standard search engines, specialized search engines like Shodan (for discovering Internet-connected devices) and Censys (for uncovering internet assets) can yield valuable insights.

B. Social Media Scraping

Social media platforms are rich sources of information about individuals and organizations. Techniques include:

Profile Analysis: Reviewing employee profiles on platforms like LinkedIn or Twitter can reveal organizational structures, technologies used, and potential vulnerabilities.

Content Mining: Searching for mentions of the organization, its products, or relevant industry topics can help identify insights into employee sentiment and potential weaknesses.

Geo-Tagging and Location Information: Monitoring geotagged posts or checking-in at events can provide information on employee movements and operational practices.

C. Domain and Network Reconnaissance

Gathering information about a target organization's domain and network can be accomplished through various techniques, including:

WHOIS Lookups: Performing WHOIS lookups to identify domain registration details, including registrant information, registration dates, and expiration dates.

DNS Enumeration: Using tools to perform DNS queries to discover subdomains, IP addresses, and other network-related information.

Passive DNS Analysis: Leveraging databases that maintain historical DNS records to identify changes and patterns in domain names.

3. Utilizing OSINT Tools

A. OSINT Frameworks and Tools

Several frameworks and tools can assist Red Teams in conducting OSINT effectively. Notable ones include:

Maltego: A data mining tool that provides graphical link analysis and allows users to visualize relationships between various pieces of information.

Recon-ng: A full-featured Web Reconnaissance framework that provides various modules for gathering OSINT from different sources.

TheHarvester: A simple tool designed to gather emails, subdomains, and names from different public sources.

SpiderFoot: An automation tool for OSINT collection that can gather information on IPs, domains, and emails.

B. Automation and Scripting

Automation can significantly enhance OSINT efforts. Techniques include:

Python Scripting: Writing custom scripts to automate the data collection process. Libraries like Beautiful Soup and Scrapy can be used for web scraping, while requests can be employed for API interactions.

APIs for Data Retrieval: Utilizing APIs provided by platforms such as Twitter, LinkedIn, or GitHub to collect relevant information programmatically.

4. Analyzing and Interpreting OSINT Data

A. Data Correlation

After collecting OSINT data, the next step involves correlating and analyzing the information. Key considerations include:

Identifying Patterns: Analyzing the collected data to identify patterns or trends that may indicate potential vulnerabilities or attack vectors.

Creating Profiles: Building profiles of key personnel, systems, and processes within the target organization to understand potential risks and vulnerabilities.

B. Threat Intelligence Integration

Integrating OSINT findings with existing threat intelligence can enhance the effectiveness of Red Team operations. This may involve:

Threat Hunting: Using OSINT data to proactively search for signs of compromise or vulnerabilities within the organization.

Contextualizing Risks: Providing context to potential threats based on historical data and known vulnerabilities in similar organizations or sectors.

5. Ethical Considerations in OSINT

A. Responsible Use of OSINT

While OSINT relies on publicly available information, ethical considerations must guide its use:

Respect for Privacy: Avoiding the collection of personally identifiable information (PII) unless necessary for legitimate security purposes.

Compliance with Legal Regulations: Adhering to legal regulations and organizational policies regarding data collection and privacy.

Avoiding Malicious Intent: Ensuring that the gathered intelligence is used solely for enhancing security and not for malicious activities.

B. Transparency and Reporting

Transparency is essential in OSINT activities. This involves:

Documenting Sources: Keeping detailed records of where information was obtained to maintain credibility and allow for verification.

Reporting Findings: Sharing insights gained from OSINT with relevant stakeholders to improve organizational security awareness and practices.

Open Source Intelligence (OSINT) techniques play a crucial role in enhancing Red Team operations, providing valuable insights into the threat landscape and potential vulnerabilities. By effectively utilizing OSINT methods, tools, and best practices, Red Teams can gather actionable intelligence that informs their engagement strategies.

Incorporating OSINT into Red Teaming not only enhances the realism of attack simulations but also fosters a culture of security awareness within organizations. As the cybersecurity landscape continues to evolve, leveraging OSINT will remain an essential practice for staying ahead of threats and building a resilient defense. Through ethical and responsible use of open source intelligence, organizations can fortify their security posture and better protect their assets and personnel.

8.2. Utilizing Threat Intelligence Feeds

Threat intelligence feeds are a critical component in the landscape of cybersecurity, providing organizations with timely and relevant information about potential threats, vulnerabilities, and malicious activities. In the context of Red Team operations, leveraging threat intelligence feeds can enhance the effectiveness of security assessments and simulations by providing real-time data that informs strategies and tactics. This chapter explores the different types of threat intelligence feeds, their significance in Red Teaming, and best practices for effectively utilizing them.

1. Understanding Threat Intelligence Feeds

A. Definition of Threat Intelligence Feeds

Threat intelligence feeds are streams of data that deliver actionable insights about threats, vulnerabilities, attack methods, and indicators of compromise (IOCs). These feeds can come from a variety of sources, including commercial vendors, open-source platforms, and community-driven initiatives. The information provided can vary widely, encompassing:

Malware signatures

IP addresses associated with malicious activity

URLs and domains known for phishing or command-and-control (C2) operations

Vulnerability information

Tactics, techniques, and procedures (TTPs) used by threat actors

B. Types of Threat Intelligence Feeds

Threat intelligence feeds can be classified into several categories based on their source and the type of information they provide:

Open Source Intelligence (OSINT) Feeds: Publicly available data sources that provide insights into known threats, often compiled from forums, social media, and security blogs.

Commercial Threat Intelligence Feeds: Paid services that offer in-depth and curated intelligence, often supported by expert analysis and enhanced reporting.

Community Threat Intelligence Feeds: Collaborative platforms that aggregate threat data shared by a community of organizations, often fostering collective defense efforts.

Internal Threat Intelligence Feeds: Data generated from within an organization, such as logs and alerts from security tools, which can help contextualize external threat data.

2. Importance of Threat Intelligence Feeds in Red Teaming

A. Enhancing Situational Awareness

Utilizing threat intelligence feeds allows Red Teams to maintain situational awareness regarding emerging threats and vulnerabilities. This enables them to:

Stay Informed About Current Threats: Continuous updates from intelligence feeds keep Red Teams informed about the latest threats and trends, enabling them to adjust their strategies accordingly.

Identify Potential Attack Vectors: Understanding the TTPs of active threat actors helps Red Teams simulate realistic attack scenarios that are relevant to their target environment.

Prioritize Security Assessments: By focusing on threats that are pertinent to the target organization, Red Teams can prioritize their efforts and allocate resources more effectively.

B. Informing Engagement Strategies

Threat intelligence feeds provide valuable insights that can directly inform Red Team engagement strategies:

Tailoring Attack Simulations: By understanding the tactics used by specific threat actors, Red Teams can design more effective and realistic attack simulations that closely mimic real-world scenarios.

Targeting Specific Vulnerabilities: Intelligence feeds can highlight vulnerabilities that are actively being exploited, allowing Red Teams to focus their efforts on testing and evaluating these weaknesses.

Developing Mitigation Strategies: Insights gained from threat intelligence can inform discussions around potential mitigations and improvements to existing security measures.

3. Integrating Threat Intelligence Feeds into Red Team Operations

A. Identifying Relevant Feeds

Not all threat intelligence feeds will be relevant to every organization or engagement. Red Teams should consider the following when identifying feeds to utilize:

Industry Relevance: Select feeds that focus on threats pertinent to the specific industry or sector in which the target organization operates.

Geographic Relevance: Consider the geographic location of the organization and potential threats that may arise in that region.

Threat Actor Profiles: Evaluate feeds that provide insights into the specific threat actors known to target similar organizations or technologies.

B. Automating Threat Intelligence Consumption

To maximize the utility of threat intelligence feeds, organizations can automate the ingestion and analysis of threat data:

Threat Intelligence Platforms (TIPs): Implementing TIPs allows organizations to aggregate data from multiple sources, analyze it, and disseminate relevant information across security teams.

Integration with Security Tools: Connecting threat intelligence feeds to existing security tools, such as SIEM (Security Information and Event Management) systems and intrusion detection systems, can enhance detection capabilities and response times.

Custom Dashboards and Alerts: Creating custom dashboards that aggregate and visualize threat intelligence data can facilitate quicker decision-making and response.

4. Analyzing and Responding to Threat Intelligence

A. Data Correlation and Analysis

Once threat intelligence feeds are integrated into the Red Team's workflow, analyzing the data becomes crucial:

Cross-Referencing with Internal Data: Correlating external threat intelligence with internal logs and alerts can help identify potential threats specific to the organization.

Identifying IOCs: Extracting indicators of compromise from threat intelligence feeds and mapping them against the organization's environment can help detect ongoing attacks.

Understanding Context: Analyzing threat intelligence in context allows Red Teams to prioritize threats based on severity and relevance to the target organization.

B. Formulating Response Strategies

After analyzing threat intelligence data, Red Teams should formulate appropriate response strategies:

Proactive Mitigation: Using intelligence to implement proactive measures to mitigate identified vulnerabilities before they can be exploited.

Incident Response Planning: Informing incident response plans with threat intelligence insights ensures that organizations are better prepared for potential breaches.

Continuous Improvement: Using feedback from threat intelligence to refine and improve Red Team operations and strategies continuously.

5. Ethical Considerations and Challenges

A. Ethical Use of Threat Intelligence

While utilizing threat intelligence feeds is essential, it is equally important to consider ethical implications:

Respect for Privacy: Ensuring that threat intelligence practices comply with data protection regulations and respect the privacy of individuals.

Responsible Sharing: When contributing to community-driven feeds, ensuring that shared intelligence does not inadvertently expose sensitive information.

Avoiding Over-Reliance: While threat intelligence is valuable, Red Teams should avoid becoming overly reliant on external data and maintain their own expertise and judgment.

B. Challenges in Utilizing Threat Intelligence Feeds

Several challenges may arise when utilizing threat intelligence feeds, including:

Data Overload: The sheer volume of threat intelligence can be overwhelming, making it difficult to identify what is most relevant.

False Positives: Threat intelligence feeds may contain false positives, requiring teams to verify the accuracy of the data before taking action.

Timeliness of Data: The effectiveness of threat intelligence diminishes if the data is not timely, necessitating mechanisms to filter and prioritize current threats.

Utilizing threat intelligence feeds is a fundamental aspect of modern Red Team operations, providing the necessary insights to enhance engagement strategies, improve situational awareness, and foster a proactive security posture. By integrating relevant intelligence feeds, automating data consumption, and analyzing threats in context, Red Teams can significantly improve their effectiveness and the resilience of the organizations they serve.

As the cybersecurity landscape continues to evolve, staying informed through threat intelligence will remain essential for anticipating and mitigating potential risks. By responsibly leveraging threat intelligence, Red Teams can not only improve their operations but also contribute to a more secure environment for their organizations.

8.3. Reconnaissance Tools and Strategies

Reconnaissance is a crucial phase in the Red Teaming process, where teams gather information about a target organization to identify vulnerabilities and plan effective attack simulations. This phase, often referred to as "information gathering," can significantly influence the success of subsequent phases in an engagement. This chapter explores various reconnaissance tools and strategies that Red Teams can employ to enhance their information-gathering efforts and achieve meaningful insights.

1. Understanding Reconnaissance

A. Definition of Reconnaissance

Reconnaissance in the context of Red Teaming involves collecting data about a target system, network, or organization with the aim of discovering vulnerabilities that can be exploited during an engagement. This phase is essential for building an understanding of the target's environment, security posture, and potential attack vectors.

B. Types of Reconnaissance

Reconnaissance can be broadly categorized into two types:

Passive Reconnaissance: Involves gathering information without directly interacting with the target system. This minimizes detection risk and can include data collection from public sources, social media, and domain information.

Active Reconnaissance: Involves directly interacting with the target system to collect information. This may include network scanning, probing for open ports, and querying services. Active reconnaissance carries a higher risk of detection.

2. Reconnaissance Tools

A. Open Source Intelligence (OSINT) Tools

Many tools are designed to facilitate the collection of information from public sources:

Maltego: A powerful data mining tool that allows users to visualize relationships between different entities, including domains, IP addresses, and social media profiles. Maltego provides a graphical interface that helps map connections and identify potential targets.

TheHarvester: This tool specializes in gathering emails, subdomains, and hostnames using various search engines and public data sources. It is particularly useful for collecting intelligence on personnel and domains.

Recon-ng: A full-featured web reconnaissance framework that provides various modules for gathering OSINT. It includes features for domain lookup, searching for email addresses, and more.

B. Network Scanning Tools

For active reconnaissance, network scanning tools can help identify live hosts and open ports:

Nmap: One of the most widely used network scanning tools, Nmap allows users to discover hosts and services on a network by sending packets and analyzing the responses. It can identify open ports, running services, and even operating systems.

Masscan: This tool is known for its speed and efficiency, capable of scanning entire Internet ranges in a fraction of the time compared to other tools. Masscan is particularly useful for discovering active hosts quickly.

Angry IP Scanner: A lightweight, cross-platform tool that scans IP addresses and ports. It provides a simple user interface and is ideal for quick reconnaissance tasks.

C. Web Application Scanners

For reconnaissance focused on web applications, specialized tools can assist:

Burp Suite: This integrated platform provides tools for testing web application security. It includes features for crawling applications, scanning for vulnerabilities, and analyzing responses.

OWASP ZAP (Zed Attack Proxy): An open-source web application security scanner that helps identify vulnerabilities in web applications. It provides automated scanning capabilities and is useful for testing during reconnaissance.

3. Reconnaissance Strategies

A. Conducting Passive Reconnaissance

Passive reconnaissance is often the first step and should be conducted thoroughly to minimize detection:

Domain Analysis: Start with WHOIS lookups to gather information about the domain registration, including owner details, registration dates, and contact information. Tools like WHOIS and DomainTools can help in this process.

Social Media Scraping: Monitor social media platforms for employee mentions, organizational updates, and other insights. Tools like LinkedIn can provide insights into personnel, job roles, and company culture.

Public Records and Data Breaches: Review public records, security forums, and data breach sites to identify previously leaked data about the target organization. Websites like Have I Been Pwned and Ghostbin can provide insights into past breaches.

B. Conducting Active Reconnaissance

Once passive reconnaissance has provided sufficient background, active reconnaissance can begin:

Port Scanning: Use tools like Nmap to identify open ports on the target's public-facing systems. This helps to understand what services are running and potentially vulnerable to exploitation.

Service Enumeration: After identifying open ports, enumerating services and their versions can reveal known vulnerabilities. Nmap can also help with service detection by using its scripting engine (NSE).

Network Mapping: Creating a visual representation of the target network can aid in understanding the topology and identifying critical systems. Tools like Nmap can help create a network map based on scanned data.

C. Information Correlation and Analysis

Collecting data is only the first step; correlating and analyzing the gathered information is crucial:

Data Organization: Organize and store the collected information in a manner that allows for easy retrieval and analysis. Using tools like Excel, Notion, or even specific reconnaissance management tools can help with this.

Identify Patterns and Vulnerabilities: Analyze the collected data to identify patterns, correlations, and potential vulnerabilities. Look for misconfigurations, outdated software versions, or exposed services that could be exploited.

Build Target Profiles: Develop comprehensive profiles of key systems, personnel, and organizational structures. This helps in tailoring attack strategies that align with the target's operational context.

4. Best Practices for Reconnaissance

A. Maintain Ethical Standards

While reconnaissance is a crucial phase in Red Teaming, ethical considerations must guide all activities:

Avoiding Excessive Interference: Ensure that active reconnaissance does not disrupt the target's operations or alert security teams unnecessarily.

Compliance with Laws and Regulations: Abide by legal frameworks and organizational policies to avoid any potential legal repercussions.

Documenting Findings: Maintain thorough documentation of all reconnaissance activities and findings for future reference and reporting.

B. Continuous Learning and Adaptation

The threat landscape is constantly evolving, and so should reconnaissance strategies:

Stay Updated: Regularly review and update reconnaissance tools and methodologies to incorporate new threats and vulnerabilities.

Participate in Threat Intelligence Sharing: Engage with community-driven initiatives to share findings and gather insights from other security professionals.

Conduct Regular Training: Ensure that Red Team members are continually trained on the latest reconnaissance techniques and tools to improve their skills and adaptability.

Reconnaissance is a foundational phase in Red Team operations, providing the critical information necessary to simulate realistic attacks and identify vulnerabilities within an organization. By utilizing a variety of reconnaissance tools and employing effective strategies, Red Teams can gather meaningful insights that inform their engagements and enhance the overall security posture of the organizations they serve.

Through a combination of passive and active reconnaissance, and by adhering to ethical standards, Red Teams can ensure their activities are both effective and responsible. As the cybersecurity landscape evolves, continuous adaptation and improvement of reconnaissance techniques will remain vital to staying ahead of emerging threats and vulnerabilities. In an era where information is power, mastering the art of reconnaissance can significantly bolster an organization's defense mechanisms against cyber threats.

9. Collaboration Between Red and Blue Teams

In the realm of cybersecurity, the battle against threats is not solely the responsibility of one team; it requires a unified effort between offensive and defensive forces. Red teams, tasked with simulating attacks, and blue teams, responsible for defending against them, play crucial but distinct roles in an organization's security strategy. When these teams collaborate effectively, they can create a more robust and resilient cybersecurity posture.

In this chapter, we will explore the importance of fostering collaboration between red and blue teams. We will discuss how a culture of open communication and shared objectives can bridge the gap between offensive and defensive strategies, ultimately enhancing the organization's ability to identify and mitigate risks. By understanding each team's perspectives and goals, both sides can learn from one another, leading to improved security practices and incident response capabilities.

We will also delve into practical methods for integrating red and blue team activities, including joint training exercises and simulations that promote teamwork and knowledge sharing. By engaging in collaborative red team exercises, blue teams can better understand adversarial tactics, while red teams can gain insights into defensive strategies and technologies.

Through real-world examples and case studies, this chapter will provide you with actionable strategies to cultivate a cooperative environment where red and blue teams work hand in hand. As we examine the power of collaboration, you will discover how this synergy can significantly enhance your organization's overall security effectiveness and resilience against cyber threats.

9.1. Establishing Communication Protocols

Effective communication is vital in ensuring a successful collaboration between Red Teams (offensive security teams) and Blue Teams (defensive security teams). Establishing robust communication protocols fosters trust, enhances situational awareness, and enables both teams to respond more effectively to identified threats. This chapter delves into the importance of communication protocols, the key components that should be included, and best practices for implementing them.

1. The Importance of Communication Protocols

A. Enhancing Team Collaboration

Communication protocols serve as the backbone for collaboration between Red and Blue Teams. When both teams clearly understand how to share information, they can work together to improve the organization's overall security posture. This collaboration allows for:

Timely Information Sharing: Establishing protocols ensures that both teams are informed about potential threats and vulnerabilities as they emerge. This allows for quicker response times and minimizes the risk of exploitation.

Feedback Loops: Effective communication creates opportunities for ongoing feedback, enabling Red Teams to refine their attack simulations and Blue Teams to enhance their defenses based on real-world scenarios.

Coordinated Efforts: Clear communication protocols help align objectives and priorities between teams, ensuring that both offensive and defensive strategies complement each other.

B. Building Trust and Understanding

Trust is fundamental for effective collaboration. Clear communication fosters a culture of transparency and openness, which is essential for building relationships between Red and Blue Teams. This trust leads to:

Improved Morale: When team members feel comfortable sharing insights and experiences, it fosters a more collaborative and supportive environment.

Better Understanding of Roles: Establishing communication protocols clarifies each team's responsibilities, minimizing misunderstandings and conflicts.

Enhanced Learning Opportunities: Open lines of communication encourage knowledge sharing and collaboration on lessons learned, creating a culture of continuous improvement.

2. Key Components of Communication Protocols

A. Defined Communication Channels

It is essential to establish specific channels for communication to ensure clarity and efficiency:

Real-Time Communication Tools: Utilize tools like Slack, Microsoft Teams, or Discord for real-time discussions. These platforms facilitate immediate communication and quick decision-making during an incident.

Email for Formal Communications: Email can be used for more formal communications, such as reporting findings, sharing summaries, and documenting lessons learned.

Incident Reporting Systems: Implement a centralized system for reporting and tracking incidents, such as ServiceNow or JIRA, to maintain a record of activities and decisions made by both teams.

B. Communication Protocols for Different Scenarios

Tailoring communication protocols to different situations ensures that the right information reaches the right people promptly:

Daily Stand-ups: Establish a routine for daily stand-up meetings, where team members can share updates on their activities, discuss any challenges, and plan for the day ahead.

Incident Response Communication: Define how communication will occur during incident response, including the roles and responsibilities of each team member and escalation paths for critical incidents.

Post-Engagement Debriefs: Create a structured approach for post-engagement debriefs to review findings, discuss successes and areas for improvement, and document lessons learned.

C. Clear Documentation Procedures

Effective communication also relies on clear documentation procedures that outline how information will be recorded and shared:

Standardized Templates: Develop standardized templates for reporting findings, incident summaries, and engagement debriefs to ensure consistency and clarity.

Knowledge Sharing Repositories: Implement a centralized repository for documentation, such as Confluence or SharePoint, where both teams can access relevant materials, findings, and lessons learned.

Version Control: Ensure that documentation is regularly updated and version-controlled to avoid confusion and maintain accuracy.

3. Best Practices for Implementing Communication Protocols

A. Foster a Collaborative Culture

Encouraging a collaborative culture is vital for the successful implementation of communication protocols:

Cross-Team Training: Organize joint training sessions and workshops to help team members understand each other's roles, challenges, and goals.

Encourage Open Dialogue: Promote an environment where team members feel comfortable sharing ideas, feedback, and concerns without fear of judgment.

Celebrate Successes: Acknowledge and celebrate collaborative efforts and achievements, reinforcing the value of teamwork.

B. Regularly Review and Update Protocols

Communication protocols should not be static; they need to evolve to meet the changing needs of the teams and the organization:

Conduct Regular Audits: Schedule periodic reviews of communication protocols to assess their effectiveness and identify areas for improvement.

Gather Feedback: Solicit feedback from team members about the communication protocols and make necessary adjustments based on their input.

Stay Informed About New Tools: As new communication tools and technologies emerge, consider their potential to enhance collaboration between teams.

Establishing effective communication protocols is essential for fostering collaboration between Red and Blue Teams. By defining clear communication channels, tailoring protocols for different scenarios, and implementing best practices, organizations can create an environment conducive to effective teamwork and information sharing.

Through improved communication, both teams can work together more effectively to enhance the organization's security posture, respond to incidents swiftly, and learn from past experiences. Ultimately, robust communication protocols are not just a matter of operational efficiency; they are a critical component of a successful cybersecurity strategy that enables organizations to adapt to an ever-evolving threat landscape.

9.2. Joint Training Exercises and Simulations

In the dynamic field of cybersecurity, effective collaboration between Red Teams (offensive security teams) and Blue Teams (defensive security teams) is critical for enhancing an organization's security posture. One of the most effective methods to foster this collaboration is through joint training exercises and simulations. This chapter explores the significance of joint training, various types of exercises, their implementation, and best practices to maximize their effectiveness.

1. The Importance of Joint Training Exercises

A. Enhancing Team Coordination

Joint training exercises facilitate communication and coordination between Red and Blue Teams. These exercises allow team members to practice their roles in a controlled environment, promoting a shared understanding of each other's tactics and strategies. Key benefits include:

Improved Response Times: By practicing together, teams can refine their communication and response strategies, enabling them to react more quickly and effectively to real-world threats.

Understanding of Roles: Joint training allows team members to understand the challenges and objectives of their counterparts. This mutual understanding fosters respect and cooperation during actual incidents.

Building Trust: Regular collaborative exercises help build trust between teams, creating a supportive atmosphere where members feel comfortable sharing insights and feedback.

B. Skills Development

Training exercises provide an opportunity for both teams to enhance their skills and knowledge, preparing them for the complexities of real-world cyber threats:

Hands-On Experience: Team members gain practical experience in handling specific tools, techniques, and scenarios that they may encounter during real attacks.

Learning from Each Other: Red Teams can share offensive strategies and tactics, while Blue Teams can educate their counterparts on defensive mechanisms and best practices. This exchange of knowledge improves overall team competency.

Scenario-Based Learning: Training simulations can be designed to mimic realistic attack scenarios, helping teams to think critically and develop creative solutions to emerging threats.

2. Types of Joint Training Exercises

A. Tabletop Exercises

Tabletop exercises are discussion-based sessions where team members simulate responses to hypothetical scenarios without the need for technical setups:

Scenario Development: Facilitators present realistic cyber incident scenarios, prompting teams to discuss their responses and strategies in a collaborative environment.

Role Play: Participants assume specific roles (e.g., incident responder, communicator) to understand how different team members would contribute to incident response.

Post-Exercise Debrief: After the exercise, teams review their responses, discussing what worked well and identifying areas for improvement.

B. Live Fire Exercises

Live fire exercises involve simulated attacks where Red Teams actively attempt to breach Blue Team defenses in real-time:

Simulated Attacks: Red Teams conduct realistic attacks, utilizing their tactics, techniques, and procedures (TTPs) to test Blue Team defenses.

Defensive Responses: Blue Teams must respond to the simulated attacks, activating their incident response plans and employing their defensive tools and strategies.

Performance Evaluation: After the exercise, both teams evaluate performance against pre-defined metrics, allowing for an objective assessment of capabilities and areas for improvement.

C. Capture the Flag (CTF) Competitions

CTF competitions are gamified exercises that challenge teams to solve security-related puzzles and capture digital flags:

Competitive Environment: Teams compete against each other to find vulnerabilities, exploit systems, and capture flags in a controlled environment.

Skill Development: CTFs encourage creativity and critical thinking, allowing team members to enhance their technical skills in a fun and engaging way.

Team Building: Working together in a competitive setting fosters camaraderie and reinforces team dynamics.

3. Implementing Joint Training Exercises

A. Defining Objectives

Before conducting joint training exercises, it is essential to define clear objectives that align with the organization's overall security goals:

Identifying Focus Areas: Determine specific skills or areas of knowledge that need to be developed, such as incident response protocols, threat detection, or vulnerability assessment.

Setting Success Criteria: Establish measurable success criteria to evaluate the effectiveness of the training exercises. This could include response times, communication efficiency, or the number of vulnerabilities identified.

B. Developing Realistic Scenarios

Creating realistic scenarios is critical for ensuring that joint training exercises are valuable and applicable to real-world situations:

Threat Landscape Analysis: Analyze the current threat landscape to inform scenario development, ensuring that exercises reflect relevant and emerging threats.

Incorporating Lessons Learned: Use insights from past incidents or exercises to shape new scenarios, allowing teams to practice responding to real challenges.

Collaborative Scenario Design: Engage both teams in the scenario design process to ensure that exercises are relevant to their specific needs and operational contexts.

C. Regular Scheduling

To maintain momentum and ensure continual improvement, joint training exercises should be scheduled regularly:

Annual Training Calendar: Create a yearly training calendar that includes various types of exercises, ensuring a mix of tabletop, live fire, and CTF competitions.

Flexible Scheduling: Allow for flexibility in scheduling to accommodate team availability and changing organizational priorities.

Continuous Engagement: Encourage teams to engage in informal training sessions or knowledge-sharing discussions between formal exercises to maintain enthusiasm and readiness.

4. Best Practices for Joint Training Exercises

A. Foster a Learning Environment

Create an atmosphere where team members feel encouraged to learn from mistakes and share experiences openly:

Encourage Questions: Promote a culture where team members feel comfortable asking questions and seeking clarification during training exercises.

Constructive Feedback: Emphasize the importance of providing constructive feedback, helping team members learn from each exercise and improve performance.

Celebrate Achievements: Acknowledge and celebrate the successes of both teams during and after exercises, reinforcing the value of teamwork.

B. Document Findings and Improvements

Documentation is critical for tracking progress and ensuring that lessons learned are integrated into future training:

Exercise Reports: Create comprehensive reports documenting the outcomes of each exercise, including findings, strengths, weaknesses, and recommended improvements.

Action Plans: Develop action plans based on exercise outcomes, detailing specific steps for improvement and assigning responsibilities for follow-up.

Review and Update Training Materials: Regularly review and update training materials based on feedback and lessons learned from joint exercises.

C. Leverage External Resources

Consider incorporating external resources and expertise into joint training exercises to enhance their effectiveness:

Consult Experts: Engage external cybersecurity professionals or consultants to facilitate training sessions and share best practices.

Participate in Industry Events: Encourage team members to attend industry conferences, workshops, and webinars to gain insights into the latest trends and techniques in cybersecurity.

Collaboration with Other Organizations: Explore opportunities to collaborate with other organizations for joint training exercises, allowing teams to gain diverse perspectives and experiences.

Joint training exercises and simulations are essential for fostering collaboration between Red and Blue Teams. By enhancing communication, improving skills, and building trust, these exercises prepare teams to respond effectively to real-world cyber threats.

Through a combination of tabletop exercises, live fire simulations, and CTF competitions, organizations can ensure that both teams are well-prepared to face the challenges of the evolving threat landscape. Implementing best practices, defining clear objectives, and fostering a supportive learning environment will further enhance the effectiveness of joint training exercises.

Ultimately, investing in joint training not only strengthens the capabilities of both Red and Blue Teams but also contributes to the overall resilience of the organization's cybersecurity posture. In a landscape where threats are ever-evolving, the collaboration and preparedness fostered through joint training exercises can make a significant difference in the organization's ability to defend against cyber attacks.

9.3. Learning from Each Other's Insights

In the world of cybersecurity, effective collaboration between Red Teams (offensive security teams) and Blue Teams (defensive security teams) is critical for building a robust defense against cyber threats. One of the most significant advantages of this collaboration is the opportunity for both teams to learn from each other's insights. This chapter explores the importance of knowledge sharing, methods for facilitating this exchange, and best practices to ensure that insights gained during engagements lead to meaningful improvements in security posture.

1. The Importance of Learning from Each Other's Insights

A. Strengthening Security Posture

Learning from each other's insights enables organizations to adopt a more holistic approach to cybersecurity. When Red and Blue Teams share knowledge and experiences, they can identify vulnerabilities, enhance defensive strategies, and build a more resilient security framework. Key benefits include:

Identification of Weaknesses: Red Teams often discover vulnerabilities and weaknesses in defenses during simulated attacks. Sharing these findings with Blue Teams allows for timely remediation and strengthens the organization's overall security posture.

Adaptation of Strategies: Blue Teams can adjust their defensive strategies based on the tactics, techniques, and procedures (TTPs) employed by Red Teams, ensuring they stay ahead of emerging threats.

Comprehensive Threat Understanding: Both teams develop a deeper understanding of the threat landscape, leading to better detection, response, and prevention strategies.

B. Fostering a Culture of Continuous Improvement

Encouraging teams to learn from each other cultivates a culture of continuous improvement within the organization. This culture is essential in a rapidly changing cyber landscape where threats evolve constantly:

Feedback Loop: Establishing a feedback loop between teams allows for ongoing learning and adaptation, enabling both teams to refine their tactics and techniques over time.

Encouragement of Innovation: A collaborative environment that values shared insights encourages innovative approaches to security challenges, driving creative problem-solving.

Resilience Against Future Threats: By learning from past experiences, organizations can anticipate future threats and implement proactive measures to mitigate them.

2. Methods for Facilitating Knowledge Exchange

A. Regular Debriefings and After-Action Reviews

Conducting debriefings and after-action reviews is an effective way for teams to share insights and learn from each engagement:

Structured Debriefing Sessions: After completing a red team engagement, schedule a debriefing session where both teams discuss what occurred, what went well, and areas for improvement.

Documenting Lessons Learned: Create a structured format for documenting insights gained during the debriefing. This documentation should be accessible to both teams and serve as a reference for future engagements.

Actionable Recommendations: Encourage participants to identify actionable recommendations based on the discussion, ensuring that insights lead to concrete improvements in security practices.

B. Knowledge Sharing Platforms

Leveraging technology to facilitate knowledge sharing can enhance collaboration between teams:

Internal Wikis or Knowledge Bases: Establish a centralized repository where both teams can share findings, lessons learned, and best practices. This could be an internal wiki, a shared drive, or a dedicated platform.

Regular Newsletters or Bulletins: Consider creating newsletters or bulletins that summarize key insights, trends, and developments from both teams. This format keeps team members informed and engaged.

Webinars and Workshops: Organize periodic webinars or workshops where team members can present their findings, share insights, and discuss emerging threats and challenges.

C. Collaborative Training Sessions

Joint training sessions provide an excellent opportunity for teams to learn from each other in a structured environment:

Scenario-Based Training: Design training sessions that allow Red and Blue Teams to work together on scenarios that reflect real-world threats, enabling them to share insights in a practical context.

Role Reversal Exercises: Consider implementing role-reversal exercises where Red Team members take on Blue Team responsibilities and vice versa. This experience helps both teams understand the challenges their counterparts face.

Joint Problem-Solving Activities: Facilitate joint problem-solving activities where both teams collaborate on identifying solutions to hypothetical or past security challenges.

3. Best Practices for Effective Knowledge Sharing

A. Establish Clear Communication Channels

Effective communication is essential for successful knowledge sharing:

Regular Check-Ins: Schedule regular check-ins between teams to discuss ongoing challenges, share updates, and foster open lines of communication.

Designated Points of Contact: Identify points of contact within each team responsible for facilitating knowledge exchange, ensuring that communication flows smoothly.

Utilization of Collaboration Tools: Leverage collaboration tools (e.g., Slack, Microsoft Teams) to create dedicated channels for discussions related to knowledge sharing and ongoing projects.

B. Promote a Culture of Openness and Trust

Cultivating a culture of openness and trust is vital for encouraging teams to share insights freely:

Encourage Questions and Curiosity: Foster an environment where team members feel comfortable asking questions and seeking clarification, promoting a culture of learning.

Celebrate Knowledge Sharing: Recognize and celebrate team members who actively contribute to knowledge sharing efforts, reinforcing the value of collaboration.

Emphasize Shared Goals: Remind team members of the shared goals of improving the organization's security posture, fostering a sense of collective responsibility.

C. Measure the Impact of Knowledge Sharing

To ensure that knowledge sharing efforts are effective, organizations should measure their impact:

Define Key Performance Indicators (KPIs): Establish KPIs to evaluate the effectiveness of knowledge sharing initiatives, such as improvements in incident response times or reductions in vulnerabilities.

Collect Feedback: Gather feedback from team members on the effectiveness of knowledge sharing efforts and make adjustments as needed.

Continuous Improvement: Use the insights gained from measuring impact to refine knowledge sharing strategies, ensuring that they remain relevant and effective.

Learning from each other's insights is a cornerstone of effective collaboration between Red and Blue Teams. By fostering a culture of continuous improvement, leveraging structured knowledge exchange methods, and implementing best practices for effective communication, organizations can significantly enhance their cybersecurity posture.

Through regular debriefings, collaborative training sessions, and the use of knowledge sharing platforms, both teams can build a comprehensive understanding of the threat landscape and develop more effective defensive strategies. Ultimately, the insights gained from this collaboration empower organizations to adapt and respond to emerging threats more effectively, reinforcing their resilience in an ever-evolving cybersecurity landscape.

10. Post-Engagement Analysis and Reporting

Completing a red team engagement is just the beginning; the real value lies in what comes next. Post-engagement analysis and reporting are critical steps that transform the findings from simulated attacks into actionable insights that can drive significant improvements in an organization's cybersecurity posture. This phase allows teams to reflect on the engagement, evaluate their performance, and develop strategies for future enhancements.

In this chapter, we will delve into the key components of effective post-engagement analysis. We will discuss how to conduct thorough debriefs that involve both red and blue teams, fostering an environment of learning and collaboration. By analyzing the tactics used during the engagement, teams can identify both strengths and weaknesses, paving the way for targeted improvements.

We will also cover best practices for creating comprehensive reports that communicate findings in a clear and actionable manner. A well-crafted report not only highlights vulnerabilities but also provides recommendations tailored to the organization's specific context. Effective reporting ensures that stakeholders—from technical teams to executive leadership—understand the implications of the findings and can make informed decisions to strengthen defenses.

Through practical examples and frameworks for analysis and reporting, this chapter will equip you with the skills necessary to maximize the impact of your red team engagements. By embracing a culture of continuous improvement, organizations can adapt to the evolving threat landscape and enhance their overall cybersecurity resilience.

10.1. Conducting Effective Debriefs

Debriefing is a critical component of the Red Team and Blue Team collaboration process. After a Red Team engagement or security incident, conducting an effective debrief is essential for extracting valuable insights, identifying areas for improvement, and fostering a culture of continuous learning. This chapter explores the importance of debriefs, outlines the steps for conducting them effectively, and offers best practices to ensure that these sessions lead to actionable outcomes.

1. The Importance of Effective Debriefs

A. Extracting Valuable Insights

Debriefs serve as a platform for teams to reflect on their performance during an engagement or incident, allowing them to extract key insights that can inform future strategies:

Identifying Successes and Failures: By analyzing what worked well and what didn't, teams can gain a comprehensive understanding of their strengths and weaknesses.

Understanding Tactics, Techniques, and Procedures (TTPs): Effective debriefs allow teams to dissect the TTPs employed during an engagement, offering a deeper understanding of both offensive and defensive maneuvers.

Learning from Experience: Each engagement presents unique challenges and learning opportunities. Debriefs enable teams to capture these lessons and apply them to future incidents.

B. Fostering a Culture of Continuous Improvement

A well-structured debriefing process contributes to a culture of continuous improvement within the organization:

Encouraging Open Communication: Debriefs provide a safe environment for team members to share their thoughts and feedback, fostering open communication and trust.

Promoting Accountability: Teams are more likely to take ownership of their performance and outcomes when debriefs are a regular part of their process.

Supporting Professional Development: Insights gained from debriefs can inform individual and team training needs, helping to identify areas for professional development.

2. Steps for Conducting Effective Debriefs

A. Preparation

Preparation is crucial for conducting effective debriefs. This phase sets the stage for a productive discussion:

Schedule the Debrief Promptly: Conduct debriefs as soon as possible after the engagement while the details are still fresh in everyone's minds. This timing helps maintain accuracy and relevance.

Gather Relevant Data: Collect data related to the engagement, including logs, reports, and any relevant metrics. This information will serve as the basis for the discussion.

Define Objectives: Clearly outline the objectives of the debrief. Determine what specific insights or outcomes the team aims to achieve during the session.

B. Structure the Debriefing Session

A structured format can help guide the discussion and ensure all relevant topics are covered:

Opening Remarks: Begin the debrief with a brief overview of the engagement or incident, including the objectives, scope, and context.

Review Performance: Discuss the performance of both Red and Blue Teams. Analyze key events, tactics used, and responses to identify what worked and what could be improved.

Encourage Participation: Foster an inclusive environment by encouraging all team members to share their thoughts and perspectives. This diverse input can lead to a richer discussion.

Document Insights: Assign someone to take notes during the debrief, capturing key insights, recommendations, and action items for future reference.

C. Identify Actionable Outcomes

At the conclusion of the debrief, it's crucial to translate insights into actionable outcomes:

Prioritize Recommendations: Identify and prioritize recommendations based on their potential impact on the organization's security posture.

Assign Responsibilities: Clearly assign ownership for implementing each recommendation to specific team members or departments.

Set Timelines: Establish realistic timelines for implementing the agreed-upon actions, ensuring accountability for follow-through.

3. Best Practices for Effective Debriefs

A. Create a Safe Space for Discussion

Encouraging a culture of open dialogue is essential for effective debriefs:

Emphasize Learning Over Blame: Foster an environment where team members feel comfortable discussing mistakes and challenges without fear of blame.

Encourage Transparency: Promote transparency by encouraging team members to share both successes and failures candidly.

Acknowledge Contributions: Recognize individual and team contributions during the engagement, reinforcing the value of collaboration and teamwork.

B. Use Technology to Facilitate Debriefs

Leveraging technology can enhance the debriefing process:

Recording Sessions: Consider recording debrief sessions (with permission) to create a reference for those who were unable to attend and to preserve discussions for future review.

Collaboration Tools: Utilize collaboration tools (e.g., shared documents, project management software) to facilitate note-taking and action tracking during debriefs.

Visual Aids: Use visual aids, such as diagrams or flowcharts, to illustrate key points and facilitate understanding among participants.

C. Follow Up on Action Items

To ensure accountability and continuous improvement, follow up on action items identified during the debrief:

Regular Check-Ins: Schedule regular check-ins to monitor the progress of action items and provide support as needed.

Review Completed Actions: In future debriefs, review the outcomes of previously assigned action items to evaluate their effectiveness and make adjustments if necessary.

Celebrate Improvements: Acknowledge and celebrate improvements that result from implementing debrief action items, reinforcing the value of the debriefing process.

Conducting effective debriefs is a vital practice for both Red and Blue Teams, enabling organizations to extract valuable insights, foster continuous improvement, and strengthen their security posture. By preparing adequately, structuring the session thoughtfully, and promoting a culture of open communication, teams can maximize the benefits of debriefs.

Ultimately, the insights gained during debriefs not only enhance individual and team performance but also contribute to the organization's overall resilience against cyber threats. By committing to this process, organizations can ensure that they are better prepared to face future challenges in the ever-evolving cybersecurity landscape.

10.2. Analyzing Findings and Lessons Learned

The debriefing process is incomplete without a thorough analysis of the findings and lessons learned from Red Team engagements and security incidents. Analyzing these insights is critical for enhancing an organization's security posture and preparing for future threats. This chapter outlines the methods for effectively analyzing findings, the significance of lessons learned, and the practical steps organizations can take to implement these insights into their cybersecurity practices.

1. The Importance of Analyzing Findings and Lessons Learned

A. Improving Future Performance

Analyzing findings from Red Team engagements allows organizations to enhance their cybersecurity measures:

Identifying Vulnerabilities: Each engagement highlights specific vulnerabilities and weaknesses in defenses. Analyzing these findings helps organizations prioritize remediation efforts.

Refining Strategies: Insights gained from analysis inform adjustments to both offensive and defensive strategies, ensuring that teams are equipped to handle evolving threats.

Enhancing Skills and Knowledge: By examining what went right and what went wrong, organizations can identify training needs for both Red and Blue Teams, ensuring continuous professional development.

B. Creating a Knowledge Base

A structured approach to documenting findings creates a valuable knowledge base:

Historical Context: Compiling findings over time helps create a historical context for understanding trends in threats and vulnerabilities, aiding in future risk assessments.

Resource for New Team Members: New team members can benefit from a well-documented repository of findings and lessons learned, accelerating their understanding of the organization's security posture.

Facilitating External Audits: A comprehensive analysis of past engagements can provide valuable information during external audits or compliance assessments.

2. Methods for Analyzing Findings

A. Categorizing Findings

A systematic approach to categorizing findings enhances clarity and usefulness:

Risk Severity: Classify findings based on risk severity, ranging from critical vulnerabilities that require immediate attention to low-risk issues that can be addressed over time.

Type of Vulnerability: Group findings by the type of vulnerability (e.g., technical, procedural, human factors) to identify common patterns and areas needing improvement.

Affected Assets: Organize findings based on the affected assets or systems to prioritize remediation efforts effectively.

B. Utilizing Analytical Frameworks

Applying established analytical frameworks can streamline the analysis process:

Kill Chain Analysis: Utilize the Cyber Kill Chain framework to analyze findings and understand how adversaries progressed through the stages of an attack. This framework can help identify points of failure in detection and response.

MITRE ATT&CK Framework: Leverage the MITRE ATT&CK framework to map findings to specific adversary tactics, techniques, and procedures (TTPs). This helps organizations better understand their threat landscape.

SWOT Analysis: Conduct a SWOT analysis (Strengths, Weaknesses, Opportunities, Threats) to assess the overall security posture and identify areas for improvement based on engagement findings.

C. Engaging Cross-Functional Teams

Involving diverse teams in the analysis process can enhance the quality of insights:

Inclusion of Stakeholders: Bring in stakeholders from various departments (e.g., IT, compliance, risk management) to provide different perspectives on findings and ensure a holistic understanding.

Cross-Team Workshops: Organize workshops that bring together Red and Blue Team members for collaborative analysis, fostering a culture of shared learning and improvement.

External Expertise: Consider involving external cybersecurity experts to provide an objective assessment of findings and offer recommendations based on industry best practices.

3. Documenting Lessons Learned

A. Creating a Lessons Learned Repository

A centralized repository for documenting lessons learned ensures accessibility and continuity:

Structured Documentation: Use a structured format for documenting lessons learned, including details such as the context of the engagement, findings, recommendations, and action items.

Accessible Platform: Ensure the repository is easily accessible to all team members and regularly updated to reflect the latest findings and lessons.

Version Control: Implement version control for documents to track changes and ensure that the most up-to-date information is always available.

B. Distributing Findings

Distributing findings and lessons learned is essential for maximizing their impact:

Regular Updates: Provide regular updates to relevant stakeholders, including executive leadership, to keep them informed about the current security posture and ongoing improvements.

Training Sessions: Integrate findings and lessons learned into training sessions for team members, ensuring that everyone is aware of the insights gained from past engagements.

Communications Strategy: Develop a communications strategy to share key findings across the organization, emphasizing the importance of learning from past experiences.

4. Implementing Changes Based on Findings

A. Prioritizing Remediation Efforts

Implementing changes based on findings involves prioritizing remediation efforts effectively:

Risk Assessment: Conduct a risk assessment to determine which findings pose the highest risk to the organization, allowing for a targeted approach to remediation.

Resource Allocation: Allocate resources (e.g., personnel, budget) to address high-priority findings first, ensuring that the most critical vulnerabilities are remediated swiftly.

Tracking Progress: Implement a tracking system to monitor the progress of remediation efforts, ensuring accountability and transparency.

B. Updating Policies and Procedures

Findings should inform updates to organizational policies and procedures:

Policy Review: Regularly review and update security policies to reflect lessons learned from Red Team engagements, ensuring alignment with the evolving threat landscape.

Incident Response Plans: Integrate findings into incident response plans, ensuring that teams are prepared to respond effectively to similar incidents in the future.

Training and Awareness Programs: Update training and awareness programs to incorporate lessons learned, ensuring that all employees understand the importance of cybersecurity and their role in maintaining it.

Analyzing findings and documenting lessons learned are vital components of the debriefing process for Red and Blue Teams. Through effective analysis methods, organizations can extract valuable insights that inform future strategies and enhance their overall security posture.

By creating a comprehensive lessons learned repository, distributing findings, and implementing changes based on insights gained, organizations can foster a culture of continuous improvement and resilience. This commitment to learning from experience not only strengthens defenses against future threats but also positions organizations to thrive in an increasingly complex cybersecurity landscape.

10.3. Creating Actionable Reports for Stakeholders

Creating actionable reports following Red Team engagements and cybersecurity assessments is a critical step in translating findings into meaningful changes within an organization. Stakeholders, including executive leadership, IT teams, and compliance officers, require clear, concise, and actionable information to make informed decisions regarding security improvements and resource allocation. This chapter explores the key elements of effective reporting, strategies for ensuring reports are actionable, and best practices for communicating findings to stakeholders.

1. The Importance of Actionable Reports

A. Facilitating Informed Decision-Making

Actionable reports serve as a bridge between technical findings and strategic decision-making:

Clarity and Context: Stakeholders often lack technical expertise; therefore, reports must present findings in a clear and understandable manner, providing the necessary context for informed decisions.

Resource Allocation: Decision-makers rely on actionable reports to prioritize security initiatives and allocate resources effectively, ensuring that high-risk vulnerabilities are addressed promptly.

Alignment with Business Goals: Reports should connect security findings with organizational goals, demonstrating how addressing vulnerabilities supports the broader mission and objectives of the organization.

B. Promoting Accountability and Transparency

Effective reporting fosters accountability and transparency within the organization:

Tracking Progress: Actionable reports allow stakeholders to track progress on remediation efforts, ensuring that responsible parties are held accountable for implementing recommended changes.

Building Trust: Transparent communication of findings builds trust between security teams and stakeholders, reinforcing the importance of collaboration in strengthening the organization's security posture.

Supporting Compliance Efforts: Well-structured reports can assist organizations in demonstrating compliance with industry regulations and standards, providing necessary documentation for audits.

2. Key Elements of Actionable Reports

A. Executive Summary

An effective report should begin with an executive summary that provides a high-level overview of findings:

Concise Overview: Summarize key findings, vulnerabilities identified, and overall risk assessment in a concise manner suitable for busy executives.

Action Items: Include a brief list of recommended action items with associated priorities to give stakeholders immediate insight into necessary steps.

Visual Aids: Utilize charts, graphs, or infographics to illustrate key points visually, making it easier for stakeholders to grasp complex information quickly.

B. Detailed Findings

After the executive summary, provide a more detailed account of the findings:

Organized Structure: Present findings in a clear, organized manner, categorizing them by severity, type of vulnerability, or affected systems.

Contextual Information: Offer context for each finding, explaining how vulnerabilities were identified, their potential impact, and any relevant background information.

Specific Examples: Where possible, provide specific examples or scenarios that illustrate the findings, making the information relatable and actionable.

C. Recommendations and Action Plans

A crucial section of the report should focus on recommendations for addressing identified vulnerabilities:

Prioritized Action Items: Clearly prioritize recommendations based on risk level, potential impact, and resource requirements. Use a traffic light system (e.g., red, yellow, green) to indicate urgency.

Responsible Parties: Assign responsibility for each action item to specific individuals or teams to promote accountability.

Implementation Timeline: Provide suggested timelines for implementation, ensuring that stakeholders understand the urgency and expected completion dates for remediation efforts.

3. Strategies for Ensuring Reports Are Actionable

A. Tailoring Reports to the Audience

Understanding the audience is critical for creating actionable reports:

Identify Stakeholder Needs: Before drafting the report, identify the specific needs and concerns of the stakeholders who will be reading it, tailoring the content accordingly.

Avoid Technical Jargon: Minimize the use of technical jargon and focus on clear, straightforward language to ensure that all stakeholders can understand the findings.

Emphasize Business Impact: Frame findings in terms of business impact, demonstrating how vulnerabilities could affect the organization's operations, reputation, or compliance status.

B. Using Clear and Concise Language

Effective communication relies on clarity and brevity:

Straightforward Writing: Use clear, concise language throughout the report, avoiding unnecessary complexity that could obscure key points.

Action-Oriented Language: Use action-oriented language when presenting recommendations, emphasizing the importance of timely implementation.

Bullet Points and Headings: Utilize bullet points, headings, and subheadings to break up text and make the report easy to scan for important information.

C. Incorporating Visual Elements

Visual aids can significantly enhance the effectiveness of reports:

Data Visualization: Use charts, graphs, and infographics to present data visually, making it easier for stakeholders to grasp trends and key findings.

Heat Maps: Consider including heat maps to illustrate areas of high risk or vulnerability, visually indicating where attention is needed most.

Infographic Summaries: Create infographic-style summaries to distill key findings and recommendations, providing stakeholders with a quick reference guide.

4. Best Practices for Communicating Findings

A. Schedule Follow-Up Meetings

After delivering the report, schedule follow-up meetings to discuss findings:

Presentation of Findings: Consider presenting the report to stakeholders in a meeting format, allowing for real-time discussion and clarification of findings.

Encourage Questions: Create an open environment for stakeholders to ask questions and seek clarification, ensuring they fully understand the findings and recommendations.

Solicit Feedback: Gather feedback on the report and presentation to improve future reporting processes.

B. Continuous Engagement

Maintaining ongoing communication with stakeholders is crucial for fostering a collaborative environment:

Regular Updates: Provide regular updates on the progress of action items and any new findings or vulnerabilities that arise.

Engage Stakeholders in the Process: Involve stakeholders in the development of action plans and remediation efforts to promote buy-in and accountability.

Share Success Stories: Highlight successes resulting from implemented recommendations, reinforcing the importance of the reporting process and encouraging future collaboration.

C. Review and Adapt Reporting Processes

Continuously review and adapt reporting processes to ensure effectiveness:

Solicit Feedback on Reports: Regularly ask stakeholders for feedback on the clarity, usefulness, and relevance of reports to identify areas for improvement.

Adjust Based on Lessons Learned: Incorporate lessons learned from previous reporting cycles to refine the structure and content of future reports.

Stay Informed on Best Practices: Keep abreast of industry best practices for reporting and communication to enhance the effectiveness of future reports.

Creating actionable reports for stakeholders is a crucial step in ensuring that Red Team engagements lead to meaningful improvements in an organization's cybersecurity posture. By focusing on clarity, prioritization, and relevance, organizations can facilitate informed decision-making, promote accountability, and enhance overall security efforts.

Effective reporting not only bridges the gap between technical findings and strategic action but also fosters a culture of continuous improvement and collaboration. By implementing the strategies and best practices outlined in this chapter, organizations can ensure that their reports lead to actionable insights and drive positive change within their cybersecurity programs.

11. Building a Resilient Cyber Defense

In an age where cyber threats are omnipresent and continually evolving, building a resilient cyber defense is no longer a luxury; it is a necessity. Organizations must not only focus on preventing attacks but also prepare for swift recovery and adaptation in the face of inevitable breaches. A resilient defense incorporates proactive measures, ongoing training, and an organizational culture that prioritizes security at every level.

In this chapter, we will explore the key principles of resilience in cybersecurity. We will discuss how organizations can integrate insights gained from red teaming into their overall security strategies, fostering an adaptive approach that evolves in response to new threats. The importance of continuous monitoring, incident response planning, and regular security assessments will be emphasized as essential components of a resilient defense.

We will also examine the role of employee training and awareness in strengthening cyber resilience. By empowering every member of the organization to recognize and respond to potential threats, companies can create a unified front against attackers.

Through case studies and actionable recommendations, this chapter will provide you with the tools and strategies needed to build a resilient cyber defense. By focusing on adaptability, collaboration, and continuous improvement, organizations can enhance their ability to withstand and recover from cyber incidents, ensuring long-term security and stability in an increasingly complex digital landscape.

11.1. Key Principles of a Robust Cybersecurity Strategy

In an era where cyber threats are increasingly sophisticated and persistent, establishing a robust cybersecurity strategy is not just an option—it's a necessity for organizations of all sizes. A well-defined strategy serves as a foundation for protecting sensitive data, maintaining operational integrity, and ensuring compliance with regulations. This chapter outlines the key principles that form the backbone of an effective cybersecurity strategy, providing a framework for organizations to build and enhance their security posture.

1. Risk Management Approach

A. Understanding the Threat Landscape

The first step in developing a robust cybersecurity strategy is understanding the current threat landscape:

Identify Threats and Vulnerabilities: Conduct comprehensive assessments to identify potential threats, vulnerabilities, and the specific risks they pose to the organization.

Prioritize Risks: Assess and prioritize risks based on their potential impact and likelihood, allowing organizations to allocate resources effectively.

Adopt a Proactive Stance: Shift from a reactive to a proactive approach in identifying and mitigating risks before they can be exploited by adversaries.

B. Continuous Risk Assessment

Cybersecurity is not a one-time effort; it requires ongoing risk assessment:

Regular Reviews: Implement regular reviews and updates to risk assessments to account for emerging threats, changes in business operations, and advancements in technology.

Dynamic Adaptation: Ensure that the cybersecurity strategy evolves alongside the organization and the external threat landscape, allowing for timely adaptations to security measures.

Integrate Risk Management into Business Processes: Embed risk management into all business processes and decision-making, ensuring that security considerations are part of the organizational culture.

2. Defense in Depth

A. Multi-layered Security Controls

A robust cybersecurity strategy employs a defense-in-depth approach, which involves implementing multiple layers of security controls:

Perimeter Security: Utilize firewalls, intrusion detection systems, and other perimeter defenses to protect the organization from external threats.

Network Segmentation: Segment networks to limit lateral movement within the organization and contain potential breaches.

Endpoint Protection: Implement security measures at the endpoint level, including antivirus software, endpoint detection and response (EDR), and device encryption.

B. Redundancy and Resilience

Creating redundancy in security measures enhances resilience:

Failover Mechanisms: Establish failover mechanisms to ensure critical systems remain operational in the event of a failure or breach.

Backup Solutions: Regularly back up data and implement disaster recovery solutions to ensure business continuity.

Incident Response Planning: Develop and test incident response plans to ensure a swift and effective response to security incidents.

3. User Education and Awareness

A. Training and Awareness Programs

Human factors play a significant role in cybersecurity. Educating users about security best practices is crucial:

Regular Training: Conduct regular training sessions to keep employees informed about the latest threats and security protocols.

Phishing Awareness: Implement programs to raise awareness about phishing attacks and social engineering tactics, providing employees with tools to identify and report suspicious activity.

Role-based Training: Tailor training programs to different roles within the organization, ensuring that employees understand the specific security responsibilities associated with their positions.

B. Cultivating a Security Culture

Promote a culture of security within the organization:

Encourage Reporting: Foster an environment where employees feel comfortable reporting security incidents or concerns without fear of repercussions.

Recognize Positive Behavior: Acknowledge and reward employees for practicing good security hygiene and adhering to policies.

Leadership Commitment: Ensure leadership demonstrates a commitment to security, reinforcing its importance throughout the organization.

4. Compliance and Governance

A. Regulatory Compliance

Adhering to relevant regulations and standards is critical for a robust cybersecurity strategy:

Understand Regulatory Requirements: Stay informed about applicable regulations (e.g., GDPR, HIPAA, PCI-DSS) and ensure compliance through appropriate measures.

Documentation and Reporting: Maintain thorough documentation of security policies, procedures, and compliance efforts, facilitating audits and assessments.

Regular Audits: Conduct regular audits to assess compliance and identify areas for improvement.

B. Governance Framework

Establish a governance framework to guide cybersecurity efforts:

Define Roles and Responsibilities: Clearly define roles and responsibilities related to cybersecurity within the organization, ensuring accountability.

Develop Policies and Procedures: Create and regularly update security policies and procedures that align with business objectives and regulatory requirements.

Risk Appetite and Tolerance: Define the organization's risk appetite and tolerance, guiding decision-making regarding security investments and initiatives.

5. Incident Response and Recovery

A. Comprehensive Incident Response Plan

Develop a robust incident response plan to address security incidents effectively:

Defined Processes: Establish clear processes for identifying, containing, eradicating, and recovering from incidents.

Roles and Responsibilities: Clearly outline roles and responsibilities for incident response team members, ensuring everyone knows their part during an incident.

Regular Drills: Conduct regular drills and simulations to test the incident response plan, identifying areas for improvement.

B. Post-Incident Analysis

Conduct post-incident analyses to learn from security incidents:

Root Cause Analysis: Investigate the root causes of incidents to prevent recurrence and strengthen defenses.

Update Policies and Procedures: Use findings from incidents to update security policies and procedures, ensuring continuous improvement.

Communication with Stakeholders: Communicate lessons learned to stakeholders, reinforcing the importance of collaboration in improving cybersecurity.

6. Continuous Improvement and Adaptation

A. Monitoring and Metrics

Establish monitoring and metrics to assess the effectiveness of the cybersecurity strategy:

Key Performance Indicators (KPIs): Define KPIs to measure the performance of security initiatives and the overall effectiveness of the cybersecurity strategy.

Security Monitoring: Implement continuous monitoring solutions to detect anomalies and potential threats in real-time.

Feedback Loops: Create feedback loops to gather insights from security incidents, assessments, and training to inform ongoing improvements.

B. Staying Informed and Engaged

Keep abreast of emerging trends and best practices in cybersecurity:

Industry Participation: Engage with industry groups, forums, and conferences to stay informed about the latest threats and mitigation strategies.

Threat Intelligence Sharing: Participate in threat intelligence sharing initiatives to enhance the organization's understanding of current threats and vulnerabilities.

Ongoing Training: Promote ongoing training for cybersecurity teams to ensure they are equipped with the skills and knowledge to address evolving challenges.

Establishing a robust cybersecurity strategy is a multifaceted endeavor that requires a commitment to risk management, defense in depth, user education, compliance, incident response, and continuous improvement. By adhering to these key principles, organizations can build a resilient security posture capable of adapting to the ever-changing threat landscape.

Implementing these principles fosters a proactive cybersecurity culture that empowers employees, engages stakeholders, and ensures that the organization remains prepared to defend against the myriad of cyber threats it faces. In a world where cyber resilience is paramount, these foundational elements will guide organizations in their journey toward a more secure future.

11.2. Continuous Monitoring and Improvement

In today's rapidly evolving digital landscape, a one-time investment in cybersecurity measures is no longer sufficient. Cyber threats are dynamic, constantly adapting to circumvent security controls. Therefore, continuous monitoring and improvement of cybersecurity strategies have become essential components in maintaining a resilient defense posture. This chapter delves into the importance of continuous monitoring, the methodologies involved, and the best practices for fostering an environment of ongoing improvement in cybersecurity.

1. The Need for Continuous Monitoring

A. Evolving Threat Landscape

Cyber threats are increasingly sophisticated and diverse, making continuous monitoring a necessity:

Adaptation of Attack Methods: Cybercriminals continuously evolve their tactics, techniques, and procedures (TTPs), necessitating ongoing vigilance to identify new threats.

Zero-Day Vulnerabilities: New vulnerabilities are discovered daily, and organizations must be prepared to detect and respond to these threats before they can be exploited.

Insider Threats: Risks are not limited to external actors; insider threats—both malicious and unintentional—can compromise security, highlighting the need for continuous observation.

B. Compliance Requirements

Many industries face stringent regulatory requirements that mandate continuous monitoring:

Audit Readiness: Regular monitoring helps ensure compliance with regulatory frameworks (e.g., GDPR, HIPAA, PCI-DSS) by documenting security controls and incident response.

Risk Management: Continuous monitoring supports ongoing risk assessments, enabling organizations to adapt to changing regulations and standards.

Accountability: A continuous monitoring program establishes accountability, demonstrating to stakeholders and regulators that the organization is actively managing cybersecurity risks.

2. Components of Continuous Monitoring

A. Security Information and Event Management (SIEM)

SIEM systems play a crucial role in continuous monitoring by aggregating and analyzing security data:

Real-Time Analysis: SIEM tools collect logs and security events from across the network, providing real-time analysis and alerting security teams to potential threats.

Incident Correlation: By correlating events from different sources, SIEM systems help identify patterns indicative of attacks, enabling faster response times.

Centralized Visibility: SIEM solutions provide centralized visibility into security events, allowing organizations to monitor their security posture effectively.

B. Threat Intelligence Integration

Integrating threat intelligence into monitoring practices enhances situational awareness:

External Threat Intelligence: Utilize threat intelligence feeds to stay informed about emerging threats and vulnerabilities relevant to the organization's industry.

Internal Intelligence: Analyze historical security events and incidents to identify trends and improve the detection of similar threats in the future.

Automated Threat Feeds: Leverage automated threat intelligence feeds that continuously update security measures based on the latest threat information.

C. Endpoint Monitoring

Continuous monitoring of endpoints is vital for detecting suspicious activity:

Endpoint Detection and Response (EDR): Implement EDR solutions that continuously monitor endpoint activity for signs of compromise or abnormal behavior.

Behavioral Analytics: Use behavioral analytics to establish baselines of normal activity, allowing for the identification of anomalies that may indicate a security incident.

Patch Management: Regularly monitor and manage endpoint patches to ensure that systems are up to date and protected against known vulnerabilities.

3. Establishing a Continuous Improvement Process

A. Regular Security Assessments

Ongoing assessments are critical for identifying gaps in security measures:

Vulnerability Scanning: Conduct regular vulnerability scans to identify weaknesses in systems and applications, enabling timely remediation.

Penetration Testing: Schedule periodic penetration tests to simulate attacks and assess the effectiveness of existing security controls.

Compliance Audits: Perform regular audits to ensure adherence to regulatory requirements and internal security policies.

B. Feedback Loops and Reporting

Establishing feedback loops fosters a culture of continuous improvement:

Post-Incident Reviews: Conduct post-incident reviews to analyze security incidents and identify areas for improvement in policies, procedures, and technology.

User Feedback: Gather feedback from users regarding security training and awareness programs to improve content and effectiveness.

Reporting Mechanisms: Implement reporting mechanisms that allow team members to share insights on security practices, helping to identify opportunities for improvement.

C. Training and Awareness Programs

Continuous education and awareness are crucial for maintaining a vigilant workforce:

Regular Training Updates: Provide regular updates to security training programs, ensuring employees are informed about the latest threats and mitigation strategies.

Phishing Simulations: Conduct phishing simulations to assess employee awareness and response to social engineering attacks, reinforcing best practices.

Encouraging Security Champions: Identify and empower security champions within departments to promote security awareness and best practices among peers.

4. Leveraging Automation in Continuous Monitoring

A. Automation of Routine Tasks

Automating routine monitoring tasks enhances efficiency and allows security teams to focus on strategic initiatives:

Automated Alerts: Set up automated alerts for suspicious activities, reducing the response time to potential incidents.

Routine Reporting: Automate routine reporting processes to ensure that stakeholders receive timely updates on security posture without manual intervention.

Patch Management Automation: Use automation tools to streamline patch management, ensuring timely updates of software and systems.

B. Machine Learning and AI

Integrating machine learning and artificial intelligence into monitoring processes can enhance threat detection capabilities:

Anomaly Detection: Use machine learning algorithms to analyze patterns in network traffic, identifying anomalies that may indicate malicious activity.

Predictive Analysis: Implement predictive analytics to forecast potential threats based on historical data, enabling proactive measures.

Automated Threat Response: Develop automated threat response mechanisms to quickly isolate and remediate threats without human intervention.

5. Creating a Culture of Continuous Improvement

A. Leadership Commitment

Leadership plays a vital role in fostering a culture of continuous improvement:

Establishing Clear Objectives: Leadership should establish clear objectives for the continuous monitoring and improvement program, aligning it with business goals.

Investing in Resources: Allocate necessary resources for monitoring tools, training, and staff to enhance the organization's security posture.

Promoting a Security-First Mindset: Encourage a culture where security is prioritized, and all employees understand their role in maintaining security.

B. Collaboration Across Teams

Encourage collaboration between IT, security, and other business units:

Cross-Functional Teams: Create cross-functional teams to address cybersecurity challenges, leveraging diverse expertise to improve overall security.

Regular Communication: Foster regular communication between teams to share insights, challenges, and successes related to cybersecurity efforts.

Integrating Security into Business Processes: Ensure that cybersecurity considerations are integrated into all business processes, promoting a holistic approach to security.

Continuous monitoring and improvement are essential components of a robust cybersecurity strategy. In an environment where threats evolve rapidly, organizations must remain vigilant, leveraging advanced technologies, adopting best practices, and fostering a culture of security awareness. By establishing a comprehensive approach to continuous monitoring, organizations can not only detect and respond to threats more effectively but also enhance their overall security posture and resilience against cyber threats.

As the digital landscape continues to change, organizations that prioritize continuous monitoring and improvement will be better equipped to protect their assets, data, and reputation, ensuring long-term success in an increasingly challenging environment. Through ongoing assessments, effective communication, and collaboration, organizations can foster an adaptive cybersecurity strategy that evolves alongside the threat landscape, enabling them to stay one step ahead of adversaries.

11.3. Incident Response Planning and Execution

In the realm of cybersecurity, the inevitability of incidents—whether they are data breaches, malware infections, or insider threats—highlights the critical need for effective incident response planning and execution. Organizations must prepare to respond quickly and efficiently to minimize damage, protect sensitive data, and maintain stakeholder trust. This chapter explores the fundamental components of incident response planning and execution, providing a framework for organizations to develop a comprehensive incident response strategy.

1. Understanding Incident Response

A. Definition of Incident Response

Incident response is the systematic approach to preparing for, detecting, analyzing, and responding to cybersecurity incidents. An effective incident response plan outlines the processes and procedures that organizations should follow when an incident occurs.

Incident Identification: The ability to recognize potential security incidents is the first step in an effective response. Organizations must employ monitoring tools and processes to detect anomalies indicative of a breach.

Impact Assessment: Once an incident is identified, the organization must assess its potential impact on operations, data integrity, and reputation.

Response and Recovery: The goal of incident response is to manage the incident effectively, restore normal operations, and prevent recurrence through lessons learned.

B. Importance of Incident Response Planning

A well-defined incident response plan is essential for several reasons:

Minimizing Damage: A swift and coordinated response can significantly reduce the impact of an incident, limiting data loss and operational downtime.

Regulatory Compliance: Many industries have regulatory requirements mandating the establishment of incident response protocols, making adherence essential for compliance.

Reputation Management: Effective incident response helps maintain customer and stakeholder trust, demonstrating the organization's commitment to security.

2. Developing an Incident Response Plan

A. Establishing an Incident Response Team (IRT)

The foundation of any incident response plan is a dedicated incident response team composed of skilled professionals:

Team Composition: The IRT should include members from various departments, including IT, security, legal, communications, and human resources, to ensure a comprehensive response.

Defining Roles and Responsibilities: Clearly outline the roles and responsibilities of each team member, ensuring accountability and efficient coordination during incidents.

Training and Skill Development: Regular training and skill development are essential for IRT members to stay current with best practices and emerging threats.

B. Incident Response Phases

An effective incident response plan encompasses several critical phases:

Preparation: This phase involves developing the incident response plan, establishing communication protocols, and conducting training exercises. Organizations should also ensure they have the necessary tools and technologies in place to detect and respond to incidents.

Detection and Analysis: Organizations must continuously monitor for potential incidents, utilizing tools like Security Information and Event Management (SIEM) systems to detect anomalies. Once an incident is detected, a thorough analysis must be conducted to understand its nature and scope.

Containment, Eradication, and Recovery: After an incident is confirmed, immediate containment is crucial to prevent further damage. This phase may involve isolating affected systems, removing malware, and restoring systems from clean backups. Once the threat is eradicated, recovery efforts should focus on restoring normal operations while ensuring that the vulnerability has been addressed.

Post-Incident Activity: Following the resolution of an incident, organizations must conduct a post-incident review to analyze what occurred, evaluate the effectiveness of the response, and identify areas for improvement. This phase often includes updating the incident response plan based on lessons learned.

3. Key Components of an Incident Response Plan

A. Communication Protocols

Effective communication is crucial during an incident. Organizations should establish protocols for both internal and external communications:

Internal Communication: Define communication channels for the incident response team and other stakeholders to ensure timely information sharing during an incident.

External Communication: Develop templates for communicating with customers, partners, and regulators. Transparency is essential, especially if personal data is compromised.

Media Relations: Prepare a media communication strategy to manage public relations and mitigate reputational damage during and after an incident.

B. Documentation and Reporting

Comprehensive documentation during an incident is critical for effective response and future reference:

Incident Log: Maintain an incident log that captures details such as the nature of the incident, actions taken, and decisions made during the response.

Post-Incident Report: Create a detailed post-incident report that outlines the findings from the incident review, including recommendations for improvement.

Regulatory Reporting: Ensure that the incident response plan includes procedures for meeting regulatory reporting requirements in the event of a data breach.

4. Testing and Exercising the Incident Response Plan

A. Simulation Exercises

Regular testing of the incident response plan through simulation exercises is essential to validate its effectiveness:

Tabletop Exercises: Conduct tabletop exercises where the incident response team discusses their actions and decisions in response to a simulated incident scenario. This promotes discussion and identification of potential weaknesses.

Full-Scale Drills: Implement full-scale drills that simulate real-world incidents, allowing the team to practice response procedures in a controlled environment.

Continuous Improvement: After each exercise, gather feedback to refine the incident response plan and address identified gaps.

B. Incorporating Lessons Learned

Each incident and exercise should be an opportunity for learning:

Review and Analyze: After an incident or exercise, conduct a thorough review of the response to identify successes and areas for improvement.

Update the Plan: Incorporate lessons learned into the incident response plan, ensuring it remains relevant and effective in addressing evolving threats.

Foster a Culture of Improvement: Encourage a culture where feedback and continuous improvement are valued, helping the organization adapt to new challenges.

5. Leveraging Technology for Incident Response

A. Automated Response Solutions

Technology can enhance incident response efficiency:

Security Automation Tools: Implement security automation tools to streamline incident detection and response, reducing the burden on security teams.

Threat Intelligence Integration: Utilize threat intelligence platforms to inform incident response actions, providing context about known threats and vulnerabilities.

Incident Response Platforms: Consider adopting dedicated incident response platforms that provide centralized management of incident response efforts, including collaboration tools and playbooks.

B. Forensic Analysis Tools

In-depth forensic analysis is crucial for understanding incidents:

Digital Forensics Tools: Use digital forensics tools to analyze compromised systems, collect evidence, and understand the attack vector used by adversaries.

Network Traffic Analysis: Implement network traffic analysis solutions to identify unusual patterns and behaviors indicative of a security incident.

Incident Response Playbooks: Develop incident response playbooks that outline step-by-step procedures for responding to various types of incidents, ensuring a consistent approach.

Incident response planning and execution are critical components of an effective cybersecurity strategy. Organizations must prepare to respond swiftly and efficiently to minimize the impact of incidents on their operations, data, and reputation. By establishing a dedicated incident response team, developing a comprehensive incident response plan, and continuously testing and improving their processes, organizations can enhance their resilience against cybersecurity threats.

In a landscape where cyber incidents are a certainty, having a well-defined incident response plan is essential for protecting an organization's assets and maintaining trust among stakeholders. By prioritizing preparation, communication, and continuous improvement, organizations can effectively navigate the complexities of incident response and emerge stronger from challenges they face in the ever-evolving cyber threat landscape.

12. Future Trends in Cybersecurity

The field of cybersecurity is constantly evolving, driven by rapid technological advancements and the ever-changing tactics of cyber adversaries. As organizations strive to protect their assets in an increasingly interconnected world, it is crucial to stay ahead of emerging threats and trends that will shape the future of cybersecurity.

In this chapter, we will explore the key trends poised to impact the cybersecurity landscape in the coming years. We will discuss the rise of artificial intelligence and machine learning, examining how these technologies are transforming both offensive and defensive strategies. From automated threat detection to advanced attack simulations, AI is set to redefine the way organizations approach cybersecurity.

We will also delve into the growing significance of cloud security, the Internet of Things (IoT), and zero trust architectures as organizations adapt to new operational models. The challenges and opportunities presented by remote work, increased digitalization, and regulatory changes will also be addressed, highlighting the need for agile security frameworks.

Additionally, we will examine the importance of developing a proactive security culture that embraces innovation and continuous learning. By fostering collaboration between red and blue teams and investing in ongoing training, organizations can better prepare for the challenges that lie ahead.

Through insights and predictions from industry experts, this chapter will provide you with a forward-looking perspective on the future of cybersecurity. By understanding these trends and preparing for them, organizations can enhance their resilience and adaptability, ensuring they remain secure in an increasingly complex digital environment.

12.1. Emerging Technologies and Their Impacts

In the rapidly evolving field of cybersecurity, emerging technologies play a pivotal role in shaping how organizations defend against threats and manage risk. As new technologies are developed and adopted, they bring both opportunities and challenges for cybersecurity professionals. This chapter explores some of the most significant emerging technologies, their potential impacts on the cybersecurity landscape, and the considerations organizations must keep in mind to leverage these advancements effectively.

1. Artificial Intelligence (AI) and Machine Learning (ML)

A. Enhancements in Threat Detection and Response

Artificial intelligence (AI) and machine learning (ML) are transforming how organizations approach threat detection and response:

Anomaly Detection: AI-driven systems can analyze vast amounts of data in real-time, identifying patterns and anomalies that may indicate security incidents. By learning from historical data, these systems become increasingly effective at distinguishing between normal and suspicious activity.

Automated Incident Response: AI can automate response actions based on predefined rules, allowing organizations to react quickly to threats. For instance, if a specific type of malware is detected, an AI system might automatically isolate the affected systems and begin remediation processes.

Predictive Analysis: ML algorithms can analyze trends in cyber threats to predict future attacks, allowing organizations to proactively enhance their defenses. By assessing the likelihood of different attack vectors, organizations can prioritize their security efforts.

B. Challenges and Ethical Considerations

While AI and ML offer significant advantages, they also pose challenges:

False Positives and Negatives: Over-reliance on automated systems may lead to false positives (incorrectly flagging legitimate activity as a threat) or false negatives (failing to detect actual threats), which can undermine trust in security systems.

Adversarial AI: Cybercriminals are also leveraging AI to enhance their attack methods, developing techniques that can evade detection by traditional security systems. This arms race necessitates continuous adaptation and improvement of AI models.

Ethical Concerns: The use of AI in cybersecurity raises ethical questions regarding data privacy, surveillance, and the potential for bias in automated decision-making processes.

2. Internet of Things (IoT)

A. Expanding Attack Surface

The proliferation of Internet of Things (IoT) devices presents unique challenges for cybersecurity:

Vulnerable Devices: Many IoT devices lack robust security features, making them easy targets for attackers. Compromised devices can be used to launch attacks on more secure systems, creating a broader attack surface.

Network Complexity: The integration of numerous IoT devices into organizational networks complicates security management. Each device introduces potential vulnerabilities that must be monitored and managed.

Data Privacy Risks: IoT devices often collect sensitive data, raising concerns about data privacy and compliance with regulations like GDPR. Organizations must ensure that data is properly secured and managed to avoid breaches.

B. Securing IoT Environments

Organizations can take several steps to secure their IoT environments:

Device Authentication: Implement strong authentication mechanisms to ensure that only authorized devices can connect to the network. This may involve the use of certificates, passwords, or biometric data.

Regular Updates and Patching: Ensure that IoT devices are regularly updated and patched to mitigate known vulnerabilities. Organizations should establish a process for monitoring and managing device security throughout their lifecycle.

Network Segmentation: Segmenting IoT devices from critical network infrastructure can help limit the impact of a compromised device, isolating potential threats and protecting sensitive systems.

3. Cloud Computing

A. Opportunities for Scalability and Flexibility

Cloud computing has revolutionized the way organizations manage their IT resources, providing scalability and flexibility:

On-Demand Resources: Cloud services allow organizations to quickly scale their resources up or down based on demand, enabling more efficient use of IT budgets and reducing the need for on-premises infrastructure.

Enhanced Collaboration: Cloud platforms facilitate collaboration among teams, enabling real-time access to data and applications from anywhere. This increases productivity but also introduces security challenges.

Cost Efficiency: Utilizing cloud services can lead to cost savings by reducing the need for hardware and maintenance. However, organizations must carefully assess the security implications of their cloud strategies.

B. Security Concerns and Best Practices

While cloud computing offers many benefits, it also presents unique security challenges:

Shared Responsibility Model: In the cloud, security is a shared responsibility between the service provider and the customer. Organizations must understand their role in protecting data and applications within the cloud environment.

Data Breaches and Compliance: Storing sensitive data in the cloud raises concerns about data breaches and compliance with regulations. Organizations should implement strong encryption and access controls to safeguard their data.

Vendor Lock-In: Relying heavily on a single cloud provider can lead to vendor lock-in, making it difficult to migrate to other solutions if security issues arise. Organizations should evaluate the portability of their data and applications when selecting cloud providers.

4. Blockchain Technology

A. Enhanced Data Integrity and Security

Blockchain technology offers unique advantages for enhancing data integrity and security:

Decentralization: Blockchain operates on a decentralized network, making it difficult for attackers to manipulate data without consensus from multiple parties. This decentralization increases resilience against attacks.

Immutability: Once data is recorded on a blockchain, it cannot be altered or deleted without consensus, providing a robust audit trail that can be invaluable for security investigations and compliance.

Smart Contracts: Blockchain-based smart contracts automate processes and enforce agreements without the need for intermediaries, reducing the risk of fraud and enhancing security.

B. Challenges to Adoption

Despite its potential, blockchain technology also presents challenges:

Scalability Issues: Many blockchain networks face scalability issues, limiting their ability to handle large volumes of transactions. Organizations must carefully evaluate the scalability of blockchain solutions before implementation.

Regulatory Uncertainty: The legal status of blockchain technology is still evolving, and organizations must navigate regulatory uncertainties related to data privacy, security, and compliance.

Skill Gap: There is a shortage of skilled professionals with expertise in blockchain technology, making it challenging for organizations to implement and manage blockchain solutions effectively.

5. Quantum Computing

A. Threat to Cryptographic Protocols

Quantum computing holds the potential to revolutionize computing power, but it also poses significant threats to traditional cryptographic protocols:

Breaking Encryption: Quantum computers have the capability to break widely used encryption algorithms, such as RSA and ECC, rendering current security measures obsolete. Organizations must prepare for a future where quantum attacks may become feasible.

Transition to Post-Quantum Cryptography: The development of post-quantum cryptography is essential to protect sensitive data from quantum attacks. Organizations should begin evaluating and adopting quantum-resistant algorithms to future-proof their security.

B. Opportunities for Enhanced Security

While quantum computing presents challenges, it also offers opportunities for enhanced security:

Quantum Key Distribution (QKD): QKD uses the principles of quantum mechanics to securely distribute encryption keys, providing a method for secure communication that is theoretically immune to eavesdropping.

Advanced Threat Detection: Quantum computing may enable more advanced threat detection algorithms, enhancing organizations' abilities to identify and respond to sophisticated cyber threats.

Emerging technologies are reshaping the cybersecurity landscape, offering both new opportunities and challenges for organizations. As advancements such as AI, IoT, cloud computing, blockchain, and quantum computing continue to evolve, organizations must adapt their cybersecurity strategies to leverage these technologies effectively.

The key to success lies in understanding the potential impacts of emerging technologies, staying informed about new threats and vulnerabilities, and implementing best practices to enhance security. By fostering a culture of continuous learning and improvement, organizations can navigate the complexities of the evolving cybersecurity landscape and build resilient defenses against the threats of tomorrow.

As we look to the future, collaboration among cybersecurity professionals, technologists, and policymakers will be essential to address the challenges posed by emerging technologies and ensure that they contribute to a more secure digital environment. Through proactive planning, innovative thinking, and a commitment to security, organizations can harness the power of emerging technologies while safeguarding their assets and data in an increasingly interconnected world.

12.2. Predicted Threat Landscapes for the Future

As technology evolves, so too do the threats that accompany it. The cybersecurity landscape is continuously changing, driven by advancements in technology, shifts in organizational behaviors, and the ever-adapting tactics of cyber adversaries. This chapter explores the predicted threat landscapes for the future, outlining the emerging trends, potential threats, and the implications they hold for organizations and cybersecurity professionals.

1. Rise of Sophisticated Cyber Attacks

A. Advanced Persistent Threats (APTs)

APTs are long-term targeted attacks aimed at stealing data or compromising systems without detection. These threats will continue to grow in sophistication:

Enhanced Tactics: APT actors will employ more complex methods of infiltration, leveraging AI and machine learning to create adaptive strategies that evade traditional defenses.

Targeted Industries: Industries such as healthcare, finance, and critical infrastructure will remain primary targets due to the sensitive nature of the data they handle and their essential services.

State-Sponsored Activities: Geopolitical tensions will likely fuel state-sponsored cyber operations, increasing the frequency and severity of APTs as nations conduct cyber warfare through espionage and sabotage.

B. Ransomware Evolution

Ransomware will continue to evolve, posing significant threats to organizations:

Ransomware-as-a-Service (RaaS): The proliferation of RaaS models will enable even less-skilled attackers to launch devastating ransomware attacks, increasing the overall threat landscape.

Double Extortion Tactics: Attackers will increasingly employ double extortion tactics, not only encrypting data but also threatening to publish sensitive information unless the ransom is paid.

Targeting Critical Infrastructure: As demonstrated by recent attacks, critical infrastructure sectors (energy, transportation, healthcare) will remain prime targets for ransomware groups, posing risks to public safety and national security.

2. The Internet of Things (IoT) Vulnerabilities

A. Increasing IoT Adoption

The proliferation of IoT devices will create new vulnerabilities and attack vectors:

Expanding Attack Surface: Each IoT device represents a potential entry point for attackers. As organizations adopt more IoT technologies, the attack surface will expand, making it challenging to secure all devices adequately.

Insecure Devices: Many IoT devices lack robust security features, making them susceptible to exploitation. Attackers may target these devices to create botnets for large-scale attacks, such as Distributed Denial of Service (DDoS).

Privacy Risks: The vast amount of data collected by IoT devices raises privacy concerns. Breaches involving IoT devices could lead to the unauthorized sharing of sensitive personal information, resulting in legal and reputational ramifications.

B. IoT Supply Chain Attacks

The IoT supply chain presents a new avenue for cyber threats:

Compromised Firmware: Attackers may exploit vulnerabilities in the firmware of IoT devices, leading to widespread breaches across organizations that use affected devices.

Third-Party Dependencies: As organizations rely on third-party vendors for IoT solutions, the risk of supply chain attacks increases. Compromised vendors can introduce vulnerabilities into customer networks.

Inadequate Security Standards: The lack of universal security standards for IoT devices may exacerbate vulnerabilities, leading to inconsistent security practices across different devices and manufacturers.

3. Cloud Security Challenges

A. Shift to Cloud-Based Solutions

As organizations increasingly adopt cloud technologies, new threats and challenges will emerge:

Misconfigurations: Misconfigured cloud services continue to be a leading cause of data breaches. As organizations migrate to the cloud, ensuring proper security configurations will be essential.

Data Privacy and Compliance: Organizations must navigate complex regulatory landscapes regarding data privacy, particularly in multi-cloud environments. Non-compliance can lead to significant legal consequences.

Insider Threats: With more employees accessing cloud services, insider threats—whether malicious or unintentional—will pose a growing risk, necessitating strong identity and access management practices.

B. Cloud Service Provider Vulnerabilities

While cloud service providers implement robust security measures, vulnerabilities may still exist:

Shared Responsibility Model: Organizations must understand the shared responsibility model in cloud security, ensuring that they take adequate measures to protect their data and applications.

Service Outages: Cyberattacks targeting cloud service providers can disrupt access to critical applications and data, affecting organizational operations.

Emergence of Cloud-Native Threats: As cloud-native technologies (such as containers and serverless computing) gain traction, attackers will develop techniques to exploit vulnerabilities specific to these environments.

4. Increased Use of Artificial Intelligence in Cyber Attacks

A. Cybercriminal Adoption of AI

Cybercriminals will increasingly leverage AI to enhance their attack strategies:

Automated Attack Generation: AI can automate the development of malware and phishing schemes, allowing attackers to scale their operations and target multiple victims simultaneously.

Social Engineering Attacks: AI-driven algorithms can analyze social media profiles and online behaviors to craft more convincing social engineering attacks, making it easier for attackers to manipulate individuals into divulging sensitive information.

Evasion Techniques: AI can help attackers develop evasion techniques that allow them to bypass traditional security measures, complicating detection and response efforts.

B. Security Solutions Utilizing AI

On the defensive side, organizations will need to harness AI to combat emerging threats:

AI-Driven Threat Intelligence: AI can analyze vast amounts of threat intelligence data to identify emerging threats and provide insights for proactive defense strategies.

Behavioral Analytics: AI-based behavioral analytics can help organizations detect anomalies in user behavior, enabling quicker identification of potential insider threats or compromised accounts.

Automated Incident Response: Leveraging AI for incident response can enhance organizations' ability to react swiftly to threats, reducing the potential damage from cyber incidents.

5. Privacy Concerns and Regulatory Challenges

A. Evolving Regulatory Landscape

As data privacy concerns grow, organizations must navigate an increasingly complex regulatory environment:

GDPR and Beyond: Regulations like the General Data Protection Regulation (GDPR) have set high standards for data protection. Similar regulations are emerging worldwide, compelling organizations to prioritize compliance.

Data Sovereignty: With regulations requiring data to be stored in specific jurisdictions, organizations must consider the implications for their cloud strategies and data management practices.

Enforcement and Penalties: As enforcement of data privacy regulations increases, organizations face significant financial penalties for non-compliance, heightening the need for robust data protection measures.

B. Consumer Trust and Transparency

Maintaining consumer trust will be essential in the future:

Transparency in Data Use: Organizations must be transparent about how they collect, use, and protect consumer data. This transparency will be critical in building trust with customers and mitigating potential backlash in the event of a data breach.

Privacy by Design: Incorporating privacy considerations into the design and development of products and services will become increasingly important. Organizations should prioritize data minimization and secure data handling practices.

Engagement with Stakeholders: Engaging with stakeholders, including customers, regulators, and industry groups, will help organizations stay informed about emerging privacy concerns and best practices.

The predicted threat landscapes for the future present both challenges and opportunities for organizations and cybersecurity professionals. As technology continues to evolve, so too will the tactics and strategies employed by cyber adversaries. To navigate this landscape effectively, organizations must remain vigilant, adaptable, and proactive in their cybersecurity efforts.

Understanding the nature of emerging threats, such as sophisticated cyber attacks, IoT vulnerabilities, cloud security challenges, and the evolving regulatory environment, is critical for building robust defenses. By investing in cutting-edge security technologies, fostering a culture of security awareness, and prioritizing collaboration between teams, organizations can enhance their resilience against the ever-changing threats of the digital age.

As we look to the future, the importance of staying informed about emerging trends and adapting security strategies accordingly cannot be overstated. Through ongoing education, investment in technology, and a commitment to security, organizations can not only protect themselves from threats but also thrive in an increasingly interconnected and complex digital world.

12.3. The Evolution of Red Teaming Methodologies

Red teaming has emerged as a vital strategy in the cybersecurity landscape, helping organizations identify vulnerabilities and strengthen their defenses against increasingly sophisticated cyber threats. Over the years, red teaming methodologies have evolved significantly, adapting to changing technologies, threat landscapes, and organizational needs. This chapter delves into the evolution of red teaming methodologies, examining the historical context, current practices, and future trends that shape this essential cybersecurity discipline.

1. Historical Context of Red Teaming

A. Military Origins

Red teaming methodologies can trace their roots back to military operations, where they were employed to simulate enemy tactics and assess the effectiveness of defense strategies. The concept of "red team" originated from military exercises, where a designated group (the "red team") would take on the role of an adversary to challenge the assumptions and strategies of the defending team (the "blue team"). This practice aimed to enhance operational readiness and decision-making.

B. Transition to Cybersecurity

As the digital landscape expanded, the principles of red teaming began to be adopted by cybersecurity professionals. In the late 1990s and early 2000s, organizations recognized the need to evaluate their cybersecurity posture through simulated attacks. This transition marked the beginning of formalized red teaming methodologies in the cybersecurity domain, emphasizing a proactive approach to identifying vulnerabilities and testing defenses.

C. Standardization and Frameworks

The evolution of red teaming methodologies saw the development of various frameworks and standards that formalized the approach:

The Penetration Testing Execution Standard (PTES): Established guidelines for conducting penetration tests, which became an integral part of red teaming practices.

The MITRE ATT&CK Framework: A comprehensive knowledge base of adversary tactics, techniques, and procedures (TTPs) that has become a cornerstone for red team operations. This framework enables red teams to simulate realistic attack scenarios based on real-world threats.

OSSTMM (Open Source Security Testing Methodology Manual): Another influential framework that provides a structured approach to security testing, including red teaming, emphasizing the importance of comprehensive assessments.

2. Current Red Teaming Methodologies

A. Threat Emulation

Modern red teaming focuses on emulating the tactics, techniques, and procedures (TTPs) of real-world adversaries. This approach involves:

Adversary Simulation: Red teams utilize threat intelligence to replicate the behaviors of specific threat actors, enabling organizations to assess their defenses against tailored attack scenarios.

Informed Testing: By leveraging frameworks like MITRE ATT&CK, red teams can map their tactics to known adversary behaviors, enhancing the realism of their simulations.

Contextual Relevance: Understanding the organization's specific environment, industry, and threat landscape allows red teams to create scenarios that reflect potential real-world attacks.

B. Red Team-Blue Team Collaboration

The collaboration between red and blue teams (the defenders) has become a key component of modern red teaming methodologies:

Purple Teaming: This collaborative approach fosters communication and information sharing between red and blue teams, enhancing overall security posture. By working together, teams can identify vulnerabilities and improve defenses more effectively.

Joint Exercises: Conducting joint exercises allows both teams to learn from each other's insights, fostering a culture of continuous improvement and collaboration.

Knowledge Sharing: Documenting and sharing findings from red team engagements with blue teams enables defenders to strengthen their security measures and develop better incident response strategies.

C. Automation and Tool Integration

The integration of automation and advanced tools into red teaming methodologies is reshaping how assessments are conducted:

Automated Attack Tools: Tools such as Metasploit, Cobalt Strike, and others allow red teams to automate various attack vectors, streamlining the engagement process and increasing efficiency.

Continuous Testing: Automation enables organizations to conduct continuous security testing, providing ongoing insights into their security posture and helping to identify vulnerabilities before adversaries can exploit them.

Threat Intelligence Integration: Leveraging threat intelligence feeds in real time allows red teams to stay informed about emerging threats and adjust their methodologies accordingly.

3. Challenges in Red Teaming Evolution

A. Evolving Threat Landscape

As cyber threats continue to evolve, red teams face the challenge of keeping pace with new attack vectors and tactics:

Emerging Technologies: The rise of cloud computing, IoT, and AI presents new challenges for red teams. Adapting methodologies to effectively assess these technologies is crucial for maintaining an organization's security posture.

Complex Environments: The increasing complexity of IT environments, including hybrid and multi-cloud setups, requires red teams to develop new strategies for simulating attacks and identifying vulnerabilities.

Sophisticated Adversaries: Cyber adversaries are becoming more sophisticated, employing advanced tactics and tools. Red teams must continuously adapt their methodologies to replicate these threats accurately.

B. Organizational Buy-In

Gaining support and understanding from stakeholders within the organization is essential for successful red teaming:

Demonstrating Value: Red teams must effectively communicate their value and findings to executives and other stakeholders, translating technical details into actionable Insights that inform business decisions.

Cultural Resistance: Organizations may face cultural resistance to red teaming activities, particularly if past experiences have led to a perception of red teaming as merely a compliance exercise. Building a culture that embraces red teaming as a tool for improvement is vital.

Resource Constraints: Limited budgets and resources can hinder the effectiveness of red teams. Organizations must allocate adequate resources for red teaming initiatives to achieve meaningful results.

4. Future Trends in Red Teaming Methodologies

A. Increased Focus on Threat Intelligence

The future of red teaming will see an even greater emphasis on threat intelligence integration:

Real-Time Threat Intelligence: Red teams will increasingly leverage real-time threat intelligence to adapt their methodologies and attack scenarios, ensuring that assessments reflect the current threat landscape.

Collaboration with Intelligence Agencies: Partnerships between organizations and intelligence agencies may enhance red team capabilities, allowing access to valuable insights and resources.

B. Integration with DevSecOps

As organizations adopt DevSecOps practices, red teaming methodologies will evolve to align with these agile frameworks:

Continuous Red Teaming: Integrating red teaming into the DevSecOps pipeline will enable organizations to conduct continuous assessments, identifying vulnerabilities throughout the software development lifecycle.

Shift-Left Approach: Red teams will focus on early involvement in the development process, providing feedback and guidance to developers to enhance security from the outset.

C. Advancements in Technology

Emerging technologies will shape the future of red teaming methodologies:

AI and Machine Learning: The use of AI and machine learning will enhance red team capabilities, enabling more sophisticated threat simulations and automating aspects of the testing process.

Virtual Reality (VR) and Augmented Reality (AR): These technologies may offer immersive training environments for red teams, allowing them to practice their skills and simulate real-world attack scenarios more effectively.

The evolution of red teaming methodologies reflects the dynamic nature of the cybersecurity landscape. From its military origins to its current role in cybersecurity, red teaming has adapted to meet the challenges posed by evolving threats, technologies, and organizational needs.

As organizations increasingly recognize the value of red teaming in strengthening their security postures, it is essential for red teams to continuously refine their methodologies. By embracing collaboration, integrating advanced technologies, and aligning with organizational goals, red teams can enhance their effectiveness and contribute to building a resilient cybersecurity framework.

Looking ahead, red teaming will play a critical role in helping organizations navigate the complexities of the digital age, providing valuable insights that empower them to proactively defend against emerging threats and safeguard their assets in an ever-changing threat landscape. Through continuous learning and adaptation, red teams can remain at the forefront of the cybersecurity fight, ensuring that organizations are well-equipped to face the challenges of the future.

Red Team Playbook: Building a Resilient Cyber Defense offers a comprehensive framework for organizations seeking to enhance their cybersecurity posture through the practice of red teaming. This playbook demystifies the complex world of cyber threats and equips readers with the knowledge and tools necessary to proactively defend against them.

Throughout the chapters, we explored the foundational principles of red teaming, including the essential skills required to build a successful red team and the importance of understanding the threat landscape. You learned how to plan and execute realistic attack scenarios, emphasizing the need for thorough intelligence gathering and collaboration between red and blue teams. The guide also provided practical insights into post-engagement analysis, helping you transform findings into actionable strategies that bolster your organization's defenses.

As the cybersecurity landscape continues to evolve, it is imperative to cultivate a culture of resilience and continuous improvement. The techniques and strategies outlined in this playbook empower you to anticipate potential threats, effectively respond to incidents, and build a security framework that adapts to new challenges.

In an age where cyber threats are a constant reality, embracing red teaming as a fundamental component of your security strategy will not only protect your organization but also foster a proactive mindset that values learning and adaptation.

Thank you for joining us on this journey through the world of red teaming. As you implement these insights into your security practices, remember that the path to a resilient cyber defense is ongoing. Stay vigilant, remain curious, and continue to fortify your defenses against the ever-present challenges of the digital age.